A NOTEBOOK FOR TEACHERS:

Making Changes in the Elementary Curriculum

Dedicated to the Memory of
Marion Bliss Finer
(1945-1989)
Teacher and Guide

REVISED EDITION

The Northeast Foundation for Children

All net proceeds from the sale of *A Notebook for Teachers* support the work of the Northeast Foundation for Children, Inc. It is a non-profit, educational foundation established to demonstrate through teaching, research, and consultation, a sensible and systematic approach to schooling.

Copyright 1985, 1993
by Northeast Foundation for Children, Inc.

ISBN 0-9618636-0-9

Library of Congress catalog card number: 87-126317

Eighth Printing May, 1997

Northeast Foundation for Children, Inc.
71 Montague City Rd., Greenfield, MA 01301
1-800-360-6332

Photo Credits:
Marlynn K. Clayton
Bill Forbes
Deborah Porter
Cherry Wyman

"The best measure of the civilization of any people is the degree of thoughtful reverence paid to the child."

Arnold Gesell

Table of Contents

Foreword   2

Introduction   4

SECTION I:
THE FOUNDATION   6

Basic Patterns of Development   7
An introductory essay on the nature of development.

Historical Background   8
Traces the influences of developmental theorists through the century and links them to the common denominators of developmental curriculum.

Understanding Age Level Versus Grade Level   10
Developmental placement and school practice—covers age levels vs. grade levels and specific developmental variations.

Behavioral Characteristics and Classroom Implications   13
Details the behavorial characteristics of children at 5, 6 and 7; and, the implications of these characteristics for the classroom. Includes narrative, descriptive charts and various examples of children's work at each age level.

SECTION II:
A PRACTICAL APPROACH   25

Developmental Curriculum: A Definition   26

The Classroom Environment   30
A photo essay of a developmental classroom for five-year-olds.

What to Teach   40
Specific curriculum resources and materials useful in applying the developmental approach to reading and writing, mathematics and social studies.

The Planning Process   45
The planning process is central to an effective developmental curriculum. This article looks closely at the appropriate expectations for planning by children ages 5, 6, 7 and how a teacher might organize the process in a classroom. Includes sample planning sheets.

SECTION III:
MAKING CHANGES   50

FIRST STEP: A Visit to a Classroom   51
An interactive narrative engaging the reader in a study of six-year-old behavior in a classroom.

APPROACHES THAT WORK: I Am Needed-The Child as Tutor   58
A narrative describing the value of children teaching children as a part of their regular school program. Helps teachers understand the immense benefit of genuine work and responsibility for their students.

The Developmental Curriculum Goes Home   61
Helping parents understand a developmental curriculum is a serious charge to teachers and administrators. This interactive article examines the joys and difficulties of parent communication.

What Did You Do in School Today?   64
A translation for parents of the many responses to their age old question, "What did you do in school today?"

A REFLECTION: When a Teacher Looks Inside   65
An essay that raises the authentic and familiar issues which all teachers face.

RESOURCES: Bibliography   67
A selected and annotated bibliography with over ninety entries. Includes specific curriculum guides from developmental programs and developmental "method" books.

POSTSCRIPT: "The Sand-Collar Curriculum"   79

Foreword to the Revised Edition

It seems fitting that we are issuing a revised edition of *A Notebook for Teachers* in the tenth anniversary year of the Northeast Foundation for Children. When we first published the *Notebook* in 1985, we were a young organization (developmentally speaking) filled with faith, dreams and aspirations, intent on making an impact on elementary curriculum and school structure. By establishing an independent laboratory school (Greenfield Center School) and a professional development center (Northeast Foundation for Children) under one roof, we sought to build a living metaphor for the merging of theory and practice.

In our formative years, we were sustained by our dreams and hard work, but would not have become visible to so many teachers so quickly without the support of the Gesell Institute and in particular the encouragement and collaboration of Jackie Haines, now Director. We owe an immense debt of gratitude to Jackie. Without her, the original *Notebook* would not have been possible.

The first edition, developed jointly with Gesell Institute, was created for use in a series of curriculum seminars and institutes for practicing teachers. Because of that collaboration, we devoted a great deal of space to the work of Arnold Gesell and the issues of developmental placement and grouping.

The revised edition acknowledges a wider spectrum of influence and many changes in the field of education. To the delight of many of us, the "clear underground stream" of progressive education, with its rich legacy in the works of Dewey, Pratt, Mitchell and others, seems to have finally flowed into the "mainstream" of American schooling. But the evolution of this movement has been surrounded by some controversy.

Based on the early field work of Gesell Institute through the 1970's, a large number of schools (about 12% by 1985) implemented "extra year" programs so that "developmentally young" children could experience successful school beginnings without the stigma of retention. When employed properly, these programs allowed for an extra year as needed, and provided continuous academic growth for children in a classroom setting with their peers or in mixed-age groupings. Such programs were often called "transition" or "readiness" programs and operated under the titles of "Pre-1st," "Pre-kindergarten," or "developmental kindergarten." The curriculum could use the best methodology of the progressive and "open classroom" movements and combine it with the knowledge of child growth inherent in stage theories of development. Here was the origin of "developmentally appropriate practice."

Unfortunately, not all schools understood how to implement these programs properly. Many programs became "dumping grounds" for special needs children, or were used for ability tracking at the kindergarten or first grade level. Some were discriminatory, placing disproportionate numbers of minority or culturally deprived children in extra year programs. While the work of the Gesell Institute genuinely sought to create an early childhood model that honored the individual needs of children and paid careful attention to developmental differences, abuses of these ideas and practices in schools became increasingly evident.

The National Association for the Education of Young Children (NAEYC) became an important critic of these practices, especially the misuses of the Gesell Screening Assessments for school entrance. NAEYC also began work on guidelines for "developmentally appropriate practices" in the elementary grades, based on their extensive experience in the preschool field and the work of progressive educators. These have helped to build interest in developmental programs nationwide.

The revision of this *Notebook*, then, has come about because we wanted to acknowledge revision in our thinking, new directions in developmental education, and a broader theoretical foundation that guides our work in child development. This revision was made possible by the thousands of teachers who have provided economic and moral support. It is for every teacher who will use it to make a change in the classroom.

Chip Wood, Director

Northeast Foundation for Children
Greenfield, Massachusetts
June, 1991

"We need to stop hurrying children. Our school days require time. Time to wonder, time to pause, time to look closely, time to share, time to pay attention to what is most important. In school we must give children the time they need to learn. To hurry through the day, to hurry through classes, grades and a timetable of achievements, is contrary to the nature of children and will do irreparable damage to their minds and souls."

Chip Wood

Introduction to the Revised Edition

(A Word from the Authors)

We—all of us who work with children—begin with a fundamental vision of teaching: a vision based on a love of children, a trust in the unfolding of learning, and a belief in the natural order of growth. This is what led us to the profession of education in the first place. However, over the years our early vision has had a tendency to get clouded by external expectations, curriculum requirements—"getting through the material." At times, it seems, we even lose sight of the child.

Fortunately, the children will not let us become myopic. Squeals of delight, giggles, tears and hugs demand recognition, refocusing our vision.

We have written this Guide to Curriculum with the sounds of children in our ears. The authors are all teachers and parents, colleagues and fellow travelers. We have experienced the joys and pains of the first year in the classroom as well as the fifteenth. We know what it is to serve on a district curriculum committee, to explain our classrooms to a new superintendent, to get ready for an open house.

This guide came to be through the natural order of things. We used these same words by Robert Frost in our first Introduction, and they seem even more appropriate today:

*Things must expect to come in front
  of us
A many times—I don't say just how
  many—
That varies with the things—before
  we see them.
One of the lies would make
  it out that nothing
Ever presents itself before us twice.
Where would we be at last if that
  were so?
Our very life depends on everything's
Recurring till we answer from within.*

Our work began in much the same place you may now find yourself—in public school classrooms, searching for better ways to reach children. Now, ten years later, some answers become clearer—from our teaching experiences and from the countless children and teachers who have shared with us their struggles and joys.

Our thoughts turn first to Marion, to whom we have dedicated this revised edition. Even now it is hard to reshape this book which she gave such beautiful form. We cannot forget the hours and days she and Jay patiently labored to bring forth the first edition.

Our deepest gratitude also goes to our ever growing number of colleagues at the Greenfield Center School as well as to the 160 children and their parents who enliven our days and from whom we constantly draw rich illustrations of the best in teaching and learning. Thanks to Deborah Porter, Terry Kayne, Bob Strachota,

Ellen Doris, Timmy Sheyda, Paula Denton, Roxann Kriete, Allison Ward, Mary Beth Forton, Susan Pelis and Jed Proujansky for sustaining the vision. Our appreciation also to Beth Watrous for her help with the manuscript as well as her dedicated contribution to the work of the Foundation and School. For production assistance, writing and editorial skill, we thank Allen Woods, who has seen this revision through. Sandra Redemske once again provided us with exceptional graphic and layout skill.

Our sincere thanks, also, to the members of the NEFC Editorial Board, especially Alan Morgan, Sharon Dunn and most especially, Steven Finer, whose proofreading and editorial wisdom have been an immense help. Finally, our love and appreciation to our families who have sacrificed so much so that we might continue to carry out this vital work.

Northeast Foundation for Children, Inc.
Greenfield, MA

Ruth Charney

Marlynn K. Clayton

Marion Finer

Jay Lord

Chip Wood

"The business of the primary grades is not to give information, but to teach the children how to get it."

Arnold and Beatrice Gesell

THE FOUNDATION

- Basic Patterns of Development
- Historical Background
- Understanding Age Level Versus Grade Level
- Behavioral Characteristics and Classroom Implications

Basic Patterns of Development

School emanates from the child. It is the creation of an environment for that child. Ideally, it is an environment that helps the child act on, understand, solidify, and build on the world that child knows.

As teachers, we are not responsible for how a child comes to school. We have no control over internal mechanisms of biological maturation, and no control over the child's environment outside of school. But we do manipulate the environment a child joins on that first day of school.

It is our responsibility to create classrooms that are respectful of children. We must build on the sequential development and needs of children, recognizing what a child knows now and what that child is ready to attempt.

A tomato seed, unless it is left unplanted and unwatered, will produce a green plant, a small blossom, and finally a tomato. Throughout time, the pattern has been unaltered— a seed, a blossom, and then the fruit. It is the same rhythm that will produce a winter day soon after the heat of summer. Nature marches through the centuries, answering an internal clock, hardly taking notice of world events. We humans develop as part of a natural rhythm, too.

We recognize these cycles of nature throughout our lives and use them to establish predictability, order that allows function. We know that if the sun is out, it's not likely to rain; that if we regularly eat too much, we will probably put on weight; and if we don't put our child to bed at a reasonable hour, the child will be cranky the next day.

And yet, in American education, we often forget what we know about children. We would never expect or require a five year old to carefully copy a complex graph, or punish a six year old for skipping on the playground. But we do expect a five year old, who is still sorting out the world, to master letters that make little sense to her. We ask a six year old, who can only count, to sit quietly at a desk adding and subtracting in a workbook. By ten, children who have never left their home town are asked to understand the government of the United States.

Through constant interaction with their world, children begin to collect, classify, and predict. They begin, from birth, to create a model, a picture of the world which allows them to go about their daily routine with some type of safety.

This need to create models, to begin routine, is identified by Piaget as an internal need to create order that allows function. It is a need of the organism, not a requirement of the outside world. As physical skills improve, the ability to interpret and classify stimuli becomes more acute. As language and thought develop, the model expands and changes to incorporate new and profound relationships.

Children, for Piaget, are always finding similarities and differences. They create sets, and change those sets as new stimuli are incorporated into their dynamic model of the world. From birth, children are building a large block replica of their world. They never tear it down and start over, but they refine and expand it, adding new levels and corridors as they mature.

Gesell, like Piaget, spoke of ordered behavioral development in children. He identified it as largely biologically determined—an internal programming that takes all children through similar, sequential development, although at different rates and in different styles.

Through years of observation, Gesell showed that children go through well-marked phases of behavioral change, but that growth does not proceed in a straight line. Development might be better described as a constantly expanding spiral. Children alternate between stages of comfort and discomfort, equilibrium and disequilibrium, consolidation and disorder. They grow during the smooth ages of 2, 5 and 10 and the unsettled ages of 2 1/2, 5 1/2 and 11.

The close-to-home child of five who loves mother's company, will be all over the neighborhood at six, ready to explore with a daring unknown at five. The helpful five, struggling to set the table, will grow to the independence of six, challenging you to even *ask* for help with dinner.

Our desire to control children does little to modify their developmental clock. For Gesell, Piaget, and other developmentalists, children develop in response to time-honored patterns of humankind—just as the tomato always comes from the seed by way of the plant and blossom.

There are intrinsic patterns to the way children grow and develop. Children are not simply the blank slate of John Locke ready to be written upon, but rather are independent, internally driven organisms interacting with their environment, growing through clear phases of development.

In the early forties, Gesell stated:

The growth characteristics of the child are really the end-product expression of an interaction between intrinsic and extrinsic determiners.

As educators—teachers, administrators, and parents—we must clearly identify our role. It is our responsibility to encourage growth by manipulating the child's environment; but we cannot manipulate development.

Children develop on their own, driven by needs and biological sequences over which we have relatively little control. We must recognize individual development and create an environment to support and enhance developmental patterns. We must ask questions that are appropriate to, and also challenge, the child's internal stage of model building.

As teachers, it is our responsibility to make sure that the extrinsic determiners which we are responsible for— the classroom, the curriculum, the materials, our own knowledge and interactions—balance with the intrinsic determiners to which children are responding.

School starts from the child. It is the creation of an environment for that child. Ideally, it will be an environment that helps children act on, understand, solidify, and build on the world they know.

7

Historical Background

For centuries, people have watched human growth and hypothesized about the miracle of development. By the mid-1700's, two theories were popular. "Preformationism" suggested that children were merely miniature adults, while John Locke had described children as blank slates ready to be filled with the writing of parents and society.

French philosopher Jean-Jacques Rousseau challenged these theories. He saw children as distinct, complex beings. "Childhood has its own ways of seeing, thinking, and feeling . . ." he wrote. "Nature . . . prompts the child to develop different capacities at different stages of growth."

By the turn of the twentieth century, new scientific information prompted debate about how children grow and think, and how they should be educated. Throughout the century, scientists and educators have continually increased and refined their knowledge. A few of the developmental theorists who have helped guide our practice are briefly described here, in alphabetical order.

Erik Erikson (1920-   )

Erikson expanded on Sigmund Freud's psychoanalytical theory of development to provide a larger view of a child's opportunities for growth. Born in Germany and trained in child psychoanalysis by Anna Freud in Vienna, Erikson moved to the United States and continued his study of development with American and Native American children.

Erikson took each of Freud's five psychosexual stages and expanded on the basic conflicts of the stage in a social environment. In his most important work, *Childhood and Society,* he described eight stages, (adding three in adulthood). His psychosocial perspective suggests that development results from an interaction between biological maturation and social forces.

For Erikson, each stage of growth is characterized by a particular conflict between biological needs and social demands (as suggested by Freud). These conflicts can be resolved by the ego (which is present at birth), depending on the social conditions and expectations of the child's world.

For example, a child in Freud's genital stage (3-6 yrs.) is struggling to become independent of parents. The child attempts this through vigorous intrusion into physical, social and mental activities. This intitiative can be encouraged with appropriate opportunities and support.

But initiative also collides with societal limits on behavior and lack of opportunities, producing guilt and a new self-limitation. For Erikson, this conflict between initiative and guilt is largely shaped by social forces, and is the center of the child's activity during this stage.

Developmental educators recognize these conflicts in children and focus, as Erikson did, on successful solutions to developmental crises.

Arnold Gesell (1881-1961)

Considered the modern-day father of child development, Gesell pioneered in many areas of research and developmental pediatrics. Educated as both a psychologist and medical doctor, Gesell established the Yale Clinic of Child Development in 1911 where he conducted extensive studies of child behavior.

Building on his detailed observations, he suggested that the determining factor in children's growth was biological maturation, although support from the proper environment was needed as well. The development of physical structures, driven by internal genetic mechanisms, is essential before certain behaviors are possible.

Gesell spent much of his life constructing detailed norms of child development which made it possible to evaluate the developmental level of a child's behavior. These norms are still used today to assess physical growth, language development, personal-social behavior, and overall adaptive behavior.

Gesell authored dozens of books: *The First Five Years of Life, The Child from Five to Ten,* and *The Child from Ten to Sixteen* are among the most well known.

Gesell was aided by a team of colleagues including Frances Ilg, Louise Bates Ames, and Janet Rodell, who founded the Gesell Institute in 1950 as a private research institution designed to continue Gesell's work. The Institute remains dedicated to Gesell's belief that "The best measure of any civilization is the degree of thoughtful reverence paid to the child."

Lucy Sprague Mitchell (1878-1967)

Mitchell's contributions to developmental education include her work in organizing a curriculum specifically centered on developmental stages and her pioneering work with what would become the Bank Street College of Education in New York.

In *Young Geographers,* Mitchell details her view of children as explorers and geographers, organizing their knowledge through ever-larger visions and understandings of their world. Learning is an active process in which children use their environment for both investigation and support.

Mitchell's active curriculum, based on children's developmental stages, is a foundation for much of the practice that builds on developmental theory. It also lays the groundwork for integrated studies across content areas. Mitchell wrote, "Content . . . is now discovered, used, related, through a curriculum of experience rather than gathered together in convenient ready-made parcels called text books."

Jean Piaget (1896-1980)

Piaget's theories about the cognitive development of children have fundamentally influenced educational theory during the last forty years. Trained as a scientist in his native Switzerland, Piaget observed children's behavior and identified principles and stages of cognitive learning that remain central to developmental education.

Although concerned with social, emotional, and moral development as well, his thoughts on cognitive growth anchor his theories. He studied children (including his own) to establish basic landmarks of cognitive development, such as object permanence (a child looks for hidden object) and conservation of quantities (quantities don't change because the shape changes).

Piaget divided child development into four basic stages and many substages that reflect increasingly complex cognitive abilities. Piaget viewed children as "little scientists" from birth, constantly experimenting with their world and changing their beliefs in response to puzzling new stimuli. They expand their world model as biological growth allows them to think in new ways. Piaget believed that infants and children learn on their own, and that they cannot be taught concepts they are not ready to understand.

For over fifty years, Piaget studied child development, writing more than forty books and hundreds of articles and addresses. No one has had a more profound effect on our understanding of children's cognitive learning. For Piaget, "Action is the basis for thought."

L. S. Vygotsky (1896-1934)

Vygotsky's basic works, *Mind in Society* and *Thought and Language,* were written in Russia in the early part of the century and only recently became widely available to Western educators. His work broadens our understanding of how children learn through language and social interaction in a supportive environment.

For educators, Vygotsky's "zone of proximal development" establishes ways to stretch cognitive learning to greater levels of complexity by realizing what a child is able to accomplish in cooperation with peers and adults. For Vygotsky, a child's development progresses through distinct stages driven by biological forces, but the environment (or "culture") is needed to spur growth to higher mental functions.

He also suggests that mastery of language is an essential tool for the child to grow into a developed member of a society, He writes, "The child's intellectual growth is contingent on his mastering the social means of thought, that is, language."

Developmental theorists have focused on different areas of children's growth and described growth patterns in different ways. But they agree on five basic principles:

1. Children mature though certain predictable stages.

2. Growth is a function of structure—a child's genetic and biological structure and the structure of the child's environment.

3. Children progress through stages in the same order, but not at the same rate.

4. There is little relationship between development and intelligence.

5. Growth does not proceed in a straight line—children alternate between states of equilibrium and disequilibrium.

These principles provide a framework for schools dedicated to the balanced development of children. By recognizing what children know at a particular point, and what they are reaching to know, schools can encourage and enhance children's physical, intellectual, and social growth.

Understanding Age Level Versus Grade Level

"What grade are you in?"

A familiar question, repeated again and again, in school and after school, on playground, after playground, on school bus, after school bus.

It is a code: "What grade are you in?"

A pecking order question.

Sometimes it is asked this way: "How old are you? What *grade* are you in?"

Yes, school policy has guided the social expectations of more than one generation of American school children and their parents.

Children begin school, of course, *by policy,* according to their birthday or chronological ages; five, on or before December 31st of the calendar year in which the child turns five. This places them in Kindergarten. Subsequent promotion to each grade (assuming normal academic growth) occurs yearly. In such a predictable sequence we easily can chart the ages of children in any grade. In most school systems children aged 4^9 to 5^9 are in Kindergarten; children 5^9 to 6^9 in Grade One; those 6^9 to 7^9 are in Grade Two.

Graded curricula were developed to match these ages. The graded curriculum for six year olds became Grade One. The graded curriculum for seven year olds became Grade Two.

Soon, however, we lost sight of the age of the children and began sequential curriculum planning. Scope and sequence charts plotted continuous growth curves based on *graded* expectations. "What's appropriate for Grade Two?" quickly replaced "What's appropriate for seven year olds?"

Today it is a challenge to find teachers' manuals that refer to the ages of the children being taught at any grade level. We are always pleased when we do hear about textbooks that account for the ages of the children for which their content is prepared.

It is, of course, possible to have a graded curriculum for six year olds. However, all too many curriculums have largely lost sight of age and grade-appropriate content. Without this perspective, graded curriculum is illogical and harmful to overall growth. The use of textbooks for social studies and science in first and second grade is a case in point.

Children at this age do not best learn about the world around them from words and pictures but rather from their own experience and direct observation.

Developmental differences in children of the same chronological age are common. Some children may be "ahead" of their chronological age in their cognitive development. Others may be younger than their chronological age in their social or physical or overall development.

Today, more and more schools are beginning to implement programs that are more "developmentally appropriate;" that is, they are matched to the developmental abilities of the children at differing ages and take into account the fact that not all children develop at the same rate. In the best programs, schools allow for academic and developmental differences, providing flexible promotion and extra time for children who will benefit from it for developmental reasons. It cannot be stated clearly enough, however, that retention, for purely academic reasons, has been found to be harmful to the majority of children. Giving children extra time in their school career can be beneficial, but must be done with great care and attention to the true developmental age of the individual child.

"Developmental age" is the age at which the child functions in social,

physical, language and adaptive areas. It can be observed by administering a developmental assessment. It can also be determined through keen observation of children in the classroom by the teacher or specialist well-acquainted with developmental benchmarks. Research has shown that developmental age can by no means always be predicted from chronological age. Some children are behaviorally ahead of their chronological age—many are below. Experience has shown that the developmental levels of any group of children do not necessarily fall on a normal bell-shaped curve. As a rule not as many children turn out to be behaviorally ahead of their age as below.

Thus, as Table 1 shows, if as in the traditional school situation children are grouped according to their chronological age, the range of developmental ages in any single classroom is astoundingly large, often as much as two and a half years.

Table 1. Comparative Ranges in Traditional School Settings
Academic Year—September - June

Grade	Chronological Age Range	Developmental Age Range
Kindergarten	$4^9 - 6^0$	$3^9 - 6^3$
Grade One	$5^9 - 7^0$	$4^9 - 7^3$
Grade Two	$6^9 - 8^0$	$5^9 - 8^3$

Teaching to this developmental range is, of course, quite difficult. As a result, some children fail. Some will repeat academically. Others will go into remedial programs. Some will become learning disabled and be placed in special services programs. Others will manage to struggle along in the middle of the group, but will never realize their full potential. Of these children, we often hear, "He could do it if he only tried."

Many children fail in school because not enough attention is paid to their developmental age or developmental ability in the classroom. Many disabilities are, in fact, school-induced disabilities. Proper attention to developmental, as well as academic, considerations not only makes curriculum planning and classroom organization manageable, it also makes it possible for children to succeed.

Contrary to popular belief developmentally young children *do not* as a rule "catch up" to their chronological age-mates. But given an extra needed year, the "gift of time," their total growth and development will continue appropriately, *given proper school planning.*

The school's role in planning for developmental differences is of utmost importance. Both curriculum *and* social or management approaches need to be considered.

The advantages of extra time for some children at school beginning should be obvious. We all have struggled with the retention of children at older grade levels—the social discomfort, the feelings of failure and inadequacy. While retention *for developmental rather than purely academic reasons* can be helpful even as late as sixth grade—we can see how much easier it is to get children off to the right start in the first place.

Developmental Variations

THE SUPERIOR-IMMATURE CHILD

Many children whose overall developmental age is younger than their chronological age show advanced functioning in the cognitive area. So many of these children have been seen over the years that they have been labeled "superior-immature." These are the children who often come to school reading and are highly verbal, but because of their overall youngness still require an extra year of schooling at the beginning of their educational careers. This is often a hard concept for parents and some educators to understand.

However, classroom experience has shown us that these children need time to allow their physical, social and general adaptive abilities to mature *while their advanced cognitive functioning is also provided maximum enhancement.* Studies have shown that overall developmental maturity is more important to later life success than is academic achievement in school.[1] "Superior-immature" children need the chance to mature in order to preserve the superior quality of their intellect and a well-rounded character. "Superior-immature" students who go on in school without extra time, or, worse yet, are skipped ahead a grade or who spend all their time in a "gifted and talented program," often have difficulty in later grades in social, emotional and physical adjustment. Many teachers have related specific examples from their own high school days to illustrate this problem. Academically successful, they found themselves socially young and emotionally unprepared for an adolescent environment.

Superior-immature children often pour all their resources into the cognitive area, but because of overall youngness can only do so by responding rigidly to the exact curriculum expectations of the school. They do all their homework, complete all assignments, do extra assigned work and "ace" all the tests. Lacking, however, is a general creativity, a willingness to experiment, to discover or to make a mistake. Their intelligence has been channeled in order to succeed with an older group of children. Often these children appear unhappy in the classroom. They may be literally afraid to make mistakes. They may complain of headaches and stomach aches, and are often tired and fatigue easily during work periods. Given proper attention these children's cognitive strengths can be allowed to flourish and expand. A full extra year at the beginning of their school lives is often just what these children need to accommodate their specific growth patterns.

Unfortunately, all too many of these children are beginning school before they are ready through well-intentioned, but misguided "early entrance" policies sometimes found in school districts. These early entrance programs, created in response to parental pressure, are nearly always guided by I.Q. levels or scores on academic "readiness" tests, rather than by measures of developmental readiness. Studies of early entrance have shown that intellectually superior children benefit by the intellectual stimulation of school, but suffer socially and emotionally and may even be later retained. As one such study suggests, "Perhaps the most prudent solutions would be to include these children in classrooms with their appropriate agemates, yet, at the same time to provide them with accelerated academic stimulation to meet their intellectual needs."[2]

THE CHILD WITH A SPECIFIC LANGUAGE DELAY

Environmental factors do affect growth and development. Children from homes where English is a second language, or where spoken and written communication is minimal, will show younger profiles on language subtests of any developmental examination. However, we must be extremely careful *not* to label these children as developmentally young.

The issue for these children is experience *not* maturity. A language delay or deprivation should be made up for by providing extra help in the regular classroom setting *not* by providing extra time in classes for the developmentally young. Close examination of the developmental profiles of these children may indeed show even, on-age development in physical and adaptive areas while language and personal-social responses are suppressed. Such children, given extra help, *will often catch up* to their agemates within a relatively short period of time. Remedial assistance, language enrichment, and special tutoring in and around a regular, age-appropriate classroom program is the best approach for the child with a language delay.

THE CHILD WITH AN ENVIRONMENTALLY CAUSED LAG OR SPECIAL HANDICAP

A child with an environmental lag is one whose normal growth and development has been interrupted or handicapped by some life event. Such events as hospitalization, lengthy separation from a parent, the immediate trauma of divorce, neglect, abuse, mal-

nutrition or lengthy illness may delay normal growth patterns. Such children, once the cause for the delay has been dealt with, are often able to "catch-up" to their age-mates and resume appropriate school progress. Again these children are not candidates for special classes. While these children may need extra time and attention in the school environment, this is best accomplished through special intervention, special teaching and social work. Ongoing observation and evaluation of these children is essential. Vigilance by the teacher is required. *Sometimes* these children will require retention and special assistance. Repeating grade level content *may not be* inappropriate for these children. The circumstances creating their lag may have caused them to skip over, or not assimilate curriculum content.

THE LEARNING DISABLED CHILD

The child with specific learning disability presents a developmental profile that makes it impossible to assign a developmental age.

Developmental observation and assessment can help to identify children who should be referred for further special needs evaluation and also help to indicate those who simply show a young developmental profile.

A developmental screening, however, does not diagnose the disability of the child. It is not a diagnostic, but a screening device. Referral for special testing and diagnosis should be the end result from a developmental screening that elicits a scattered and disorganized pattern of growth.

THE DIFFERENCE BETWEEN BOYS AND GIRLS

School entrance policy and grade placement unfortunately does not generally take into account what we know about the growth differences between boys and girls. While both boys and girls show a span of developmental differences, boys tend to be on the average six months younger than girls at school entrance. As Soderman has pointed out, "The excellent research in brain growth periodization, which provides further biological support for the work of Piaget and Gesell substantiates the importance of recognizing changing structures."[3]

"In the early years," she emphasizes, "boys may be 6-18 months behind girls in moving through these structural changes. Our failure to apply in the classroom what we have substantiated through research is evident in the wreckages we attempt to mop up in our secondary schools; boys outnumber girls 13-1 in remedial classes and as high as 8-1 in classes for the emotionally impaired."[4]

Recent research suggests that at least some of these differences may also be due to the differing responses given to boys and girls by teachers based on gender and cultural stereotypes.

DEVELOPMENT AND INTELLIGENCE

The relationship between rate of growth and intellectual ability is one of the most misunderstood areas in education and child development.

Largely because of our society's preoccupation with achievement and success, we have come to equate intelligence in young children with early skill acquisition, early academic performance, and advancement.

TO THE BEST OR OUR KNOWLEDGE THERE IS RELATIVELY LITTLE RELATIONSHIP BETWEEN DEVELOPMENT AND INTELLIGENCE.

Some of the very brightest children, those whose I.Q.'s make them eligible for the gifted and talented programs, are also those whose rate of overall growth is progressing more slowly than their age-mates. These are the "superior-immature" children we have already mentioned who desperately need more time in a school setting to consolidate their brilliance. Perhaps just because they are more gifted intellectually they require more time to sort, balance and integrate their complex mental operations with their personality, social behavior and physical beings.

Other children, of average intelligence, may develop more rapidly and more comfortably if placed with children their own age. These children show "on-age" growth patterns with a range of intellectual abilities. Children with low I.Q.'s and questionable achievement projections may also develop with normative growth patterns. Essentially, we have found the same pattern of growth in children *of all intellectual levels,* that is—some on-age, a rare few above, and some functioning at a younger developmental age than their chronological age-mates.

[1]Norman A. and Lois Theis-Sprinthall, "The Need for a Theoretical Framework in Educating Teachers," in *The Education of Teachers, A Look Ahead,* Howey and Gardner, eds. (Longman, 1983), p. 79.

[2]Ann Obrzut, Bret Nelson and John Obrzut, "Early School Entrance for Intellectually Superior Children: an analysis," *Psychology in the Schools,* Vol. 21, January 1984, pp. 71-77.

[3]Anne K. Soderman, "Formal Education for Four Year Olds? That Depends...," *Young Children,* July 1984, pp. 12-13.

[4]Soderman, "Formal Education for Four Year Olds?...," pp. 15-16.

Behavioral Characteristics and Classroom Implications

Classroom procedure can be greatly improved by attending to children's growth patterns. Developmental theory helps us predict certain behaviors based on our knowledge of the stages of growth children pass through. These stages have been identified through repeated, clinical observations and normative research.

- All normally developing children pass through highly similar stages of growth and development.
- Children pass through these stages in very much the same sequence.
- Children do not pass through these stages at the same rate.
- The rate of development is determined by:
  —the neuro-motor growth of the child;
  —the child's interaction with the environment;
  —the environment's influence on the child;
  —the personality of the child.
- Stages of development are marked by a dynamic struggle between forces of equilibrium and disequilibrium in the child.
- *Adaptive behavior* is the constructive activity of the child. It is contingent on the child's ability to profit by past experience and to initiate new experience.
- In each stage the child uses *adaptive behavior* to acquire new skills, knowledge, and ways of behaving.
- Dramatic growth and new patterns of behavior and learning are most often experienced by the child in transitional stages or stages of disequilibrium.
- Periods of equilibrium allow children to consolidate their growth, learning and behavior.

Behavioral Characteristics of Young Children (Ages 5, 6 and 7)

The behavior of five-, six- and seven-year-old children is clearly identifiable by certain typical characteristics. Before we present a full and systematic description of behavior at these ages, we will briefly describe the characteristic behavior of the four year old. We do this for two special reasons. One is that certainly some number of the five year olds that any teacher meets with may be still behaving like the typical four.

It is important to recognize behavior for what it is and to appreciate that it is merely "young" and not peculiar.

The second reason we include this material is that some readers may live in states which are contemplating pushing kindergarten down to the four-year-old level. This description, brief as it is, will hopefully suggest how unsuitable it is even to contemplate kindergarten for four year olds.

The Four Year Old

The typical four-year-old tends to be substantially out-of-bounds. Physically, children run and jump, hit and kick, cover much ground, find it hard to remain in one spot. Emotionally they cry too hard and laugh too loud, at least from some people's point of view. Language leaves something to be desired: "Jesus Christ" and "you old wee-wee-pants" are the type of comments which prevail.

Most fours are not ready to sit quietly for any prolonged period. In school, active gross motor play is the preferred activity for many, preferably out of doors. They love the slide and the jungle gym; love to pull and tug at large boxes and blocks; love to make large and everchanging block structures. They love to dig, ride their tricycles, do anything which will exercise their large muscles.

And for many, imaginative play prevails—imaginative play which they themselves produce with little supervision from the teacher. They

like to play house, store and airplane; they like to be airline pilots, nurses, doctors or giants in caves. They love dressing up. Socializing and learning to get on with others may be the favorite and most important activity. Though many enjoy being read to, looking at books or taking part in rhythm games, few are ready for any sustained fine motor activity or work with letters and numbers such as even the most liberal and non-academic kindergarten tends to require.

The Five Year Old

"Childhood is a time of great happiness and great unhappiness— there is not much middle ground."
Caroline Pratt, 1948

Five is a time of great happiness, of equilibrium. Life is "good" as the five year old will tell you. Behavior is smooth, even and literal. The five-year-old's primary objective in life is to please the significant adults in their lives. They are constantly asking, "Mom, can I set the table? Can I put away the socks?" At school five year olds also ask permission. "Teacher, can I use these markers? Teacher, is this how you do it? How much can I use, teacher?"

The five year old needs the release of the adult to make transitions, move from task to task. Visually this age shows strong ocular fixation, often getting "stuck" in the near field of vision on a specific object or activity. Lacking the ability to sweep eyes laterally left to right and back right to left, most five year olds are not ready for the rigors of formal reading instruction.

The young five year old is in a period of consolidation, resting from the exuberant, out-of-bounds behavior of four. At four the child exaggerated, told long stories, talked constantly and was always in motion. At five, the child is highly literal and exact. One word answers, "good" and "fine" replace elaborate explanations.

Five year olds are not selfish, but are at the center of their own universe and find it hard to see the world from any other point of view. This, also, often makes it impossible for children to complete a given task except in the one way they know—their way. How-

THE FIVE YEAR OLD—BEHAVIORAL CHARACTERISTICS*

PHYSICAL	LANGUAGE	PERSONAL—SOCIAL	ADAPTIVE
• Ocular fixation near point vision • Centered on task • Gross motor control improving • Pincer grasp with pencil • Falls out of chair sideways • Paces self well • Active but can inhibit	• Literal, succinct • "play" and "good" favorite words • Needs release from adult "Can I...?" • Fantasy is more active, less verbal • Does not communicate about school at home • Thinks outloud	• Likes to help; cooperative • Wants to be good • Needs approval • Dependent on authority; wants to be told what to do, but also finds it difficult to see things from another's viewpoint	• Likes to copy • Literal behavior; often only one way to do things • Bound cognitively by sight and senses • Animistic (inanimate objects have life, movement) • Learns best through play and own action • Does not yet think logically

*Tabular material for behavioral characteristics in this chapter is adapted from Frances Ilg, *Scoring Notes: The Developmental Examination* (New Haven, CT., 1965)

THE FIVE YEAR OLD—CLASSROOM IMPLICATIONS

The behavioral characteristics of children at any age provide clues to strategies in the classroom.
The literal five year old needs the teacher's focused attention.

Vision	• Because children have not established ocular pursuit, left to right, they will tend to focus on one word at a time. • Teachers need to be aware that children will often lose their place looking at print, both in books and on the board. • Children will have difficulty copying from a blackboard or chart stand. • Children who have started to read will often need a pointer or a finger to keep their place. • Reversals of letters and numbers, though few, need to be accepted, not corrected. • Children will sometimes get "stuck" on one task for a considerable period.
Fine-Motor	• Manuscript printing can be introduced, but children should not be expected to stay within the lines. • Spacing of letters and numbers will be inconsistent.
Self-Control	• Teachers can expect children to work at quiet, sitting activities for 15-20 minutes at a time. • Children often need teacher to release them to the next task, though they are able to pace themselves well with a given task.
Language Development	• Teachers need to expect and allow children to think outloud; language often directs action of the child: "I am going to move the truck!" preceding the action. • Dramatic play through a housekeeping corner or dramatic play area is essential to language development, allowing children to express thoughts through action.
Personal-Social Behavior	• Consistent guidelines and carefully planned structure help children feel safe in the classroom. Children need to be allowed to make choices about the use of their time within the established structure. • Teachers need to be aware of children's need to touch base frequently. • Praise is an important "release mechanism" for children to move on to a next task. • Teachers need to understand and accept children's seemingly illogical understandings of cause and effect in the physical world (i.e., "It's raining 'cause the sun is crying"), but teachers do not need to *agree* with children's answers.
Child's Point of View	• Children are seldom able to see things from another's point of view.
Literal Focus	• Teachers need to allow for much repetitive behavior in the classroom. Stories, poems, songs and games should be repeated, sometimes with minor variations. Patterning in math, science and daily scheduling is important.

ever, children at this age *do* accept adult rules as absolute and unbendable.

The Five and One Half Year Old

At five and a half there is a marked transition to imbalance—the disequilibrium of a break-up stage. Visual and auditory confusions evidence themselves in the typical letter and number reversals of this age. The child is not sure which way things go—and says so! "Yes and No," replaces "YES." An occasional "NO!" reminds us of the last break-up stage at 2½. The child at this age is testing limits, beginning to question the absolute authority of the adult.

Where fives could sit still and wait their turn, at five and a half wiggles are the order of the day and it is not uncommon to see children frequently falling sideways out of their chairs (at six they will fall over backwards).

As children move toward six their language becomes more differentiated and complex.

Behavior at this age is also complex. Children can be playing well one moment and be arguing the next. They can delight in independent activity or become instantly dependent on adult intervention. Sometimes they dawdle, sometimes they rush. At five and a half they are in a major transition period. Initiative drives them forward. The more they can do on their own, the stronger they feel. However, failure at any task may produce a strong sense of guilt. The balance between initiative and guilt provides the child with a feeling of purpose and worth. This purposefulness allows them to venture on into a lengthy period of industriousness between the ages of six and eleven.

What is especially important to remember about all five year olds is that they do not think the same way about the world as adults do. Cause and effect are not explained through logic but rather through intuition. Thought which appears illogical is really prelogical. ("I go to sleep because it's night.") In this prelude to logical thinking, children are not yet able to complete mental operations through even the simplest abstractions. Bound by the senses, by what they can see, children must act on one thing at a time.

THE FIVE AND ONE HALF YEAR OLD—BEHAVIORAL CHARACTERISTICS

PHYSICAL	LANGUAGE	PERSONAL-SOCIAL	ADAPTIVE
• Visual and auditory confusion • Reversals common • Physically restless • Awkward fine motor • Variable pencil grasp • Tilts head to nondominant side • Hand "gets tired" from firm grip • Often stands up to do work • Tires quickly	• Equivocates—sometimes yes, sometimes no • Elaborates and differentiates in answer to questions • Verbal answers may not equal cognitive understanding; more words than ideas • Auditory reversals (answers first what was heard last)	• Oppositional, not sure whether to be good or naughty • Insecure with feelings • Testing authority, limits • Tentative • Complains • Temper tantrums; striking out • Wonderful at home, terrible at school or vice-versa	• Makes lots of mistakes; recognizes some • Shows initiative • Trial and error learning • Learns well from direct experience

---

THE FIVE AND ONE HALF YEAR OLD—CLASSROOM IMPLICATIONS

Many of the characteristics of five, of course, carry over to five and a half. However, at this "break-up" stage or stage of disequilibrium certain specific implications present themselves.

Vision and Fine Motor Ability	• Printing will tend to be less neat than at five and with more reversals. • Pencil "grips" sometimes help children with overfirm grasp at this age. • Reversals of letters and numbers are at their peak; reading and writing tasks can be extremely difficult and frustrating.
Gross Motor Ability	• Children begin to need more physical activity though they do not always respond with good attention in structured gym class. • Children tire quickly, sometimes necessitating shorter work periods than at five.
Cognitive Growth	• Language still initiates action; children begin to explain in more detail. • Teachers need to provide many avenues for children to express what they know (i.e., blocks, paints, arts and crafts). • Teachers need to allow children time to try out their own ways of doing things even when they sometimes get the wrong answers. Teachers should be constantly validating children's initiative when evident.
Personal-Social Behavior	• Consistent rules and discipline are even more necessary than at five, and because children are testing limits more, *too* harsh discipline, especially for mistakes, can be devastating. • The use of frequent questioning and redirecting by the teacher works better now than at five.

The Six Year Old

"The eruption of the sixth-year molar marks a transition period which accentuates inherent differences in developmental patterns. To meet these differences the induction of the preschool child needs to be made more adaptive."

Arnold Gesell, 1940

Six year olds are in a "growth spurt." Physical, emotional and cognitive development is marked by rapid and dramatic change.

The body of the six year old is growing rapidly. Tooth eruption is continuous; take note of chewed pencils, papers and workbook edges in the first grade. Visual development is coming under control; there is now good ocular pursuit, allowing for easy introduction of beginning reading tasks. Rapid physical growth is mirrored in rapid physical activity. Children are constantly in a hurry, rushing to be finished. They love to do their assignments but are decidedly more interested in process than in the final product. School work, therefore, tends to be sloppy or erratic. There is great interest in being first, in doing the most work. There are often extremes. Children who cannot be first may gladly be last; dawdling can be a favorite pastime. Along with great bursts of energy go periods of fatigue. Illnesses are also frequent.

The importance of friends now equals the importance of parents and teachers in the child's social development. Talking, along with teething, is a physical *and* social pastime. Classrooms full of six year olds are busy, noisy places. Talking, humming, whistling, bustling are the order of the day.

"Industrious" describes the overall behavior of the child at six. The child is now as interested in the completion of various work tasks as in the spontaneous enjoyment of play. Children delight in cooperative projects, activities and tasks. No job is too big, no mountain too high. However, eyes can be bigger than stomachs and sixes risk an overpowering sense of inadequacy and inferiority as they tackle new frontiers. The child is ordering and structuring the world in new ways. An ounce of praise for the six year old produces a radiant smile, hugs and excitement. An ounce of condemnation produces tears and withdrawal.

It is at six that most children begin a major transition in their intellectual growth. The child now begins to approach the world logically for the first time. Concepts begin to be organized in a symbolic manner through understandable systems and approaches. Prior to this time the child is unable to accommodate an adult view of reality and generally does not believe adult explanations of cause and effect.

The beginning of reasoning is marked by the child's ability to identify differences, compensate for differences and reverse an idea through mental activity. Thus, two equal balls of clay will not appear as different quantities to six year olds when one has been rolled out into a snake-like shape before their eyes. Young children will not be able to compensate for the difference, nor reverse the process mentally. They may not even be truly able to identify the difference.

The difference between the five year old and six year old is striking and dramatic. The shift in cognitive development is accompanied by a shift in reasoning, an understanding of cause and effect in the natural world (e.g., what makes the clouds move) and a widening vision which allows them to see another's point of view and to consider rules and conduct more relativistically.

The eagerness, curiosity, imagination, drive, and enthusiasm of the six year old is perhaps never again matched in quantity or intensity during the life span. In many ways this is the learning moment, the turning point, the opportunity captured or lost, the door opened or closed, for it is here the child is truly ready for the world of learning.

THE SIX YEAR OLD—BEHAVIORAL CHARACTERISTICS

PHYSICAL	LANGUAGE	PERSONAL-SOCIAL	ADAPTIVE
• Good ocular pursuit • More aware of hand as tool • Sloppy; in a hurry; speed is a benchmark of 6 • Noisy in classroom • Falls backwards out of chairs • Learning to distinguish left from right • Oral activity; chews pencils, bites fingernails, chews hair (teething) • Easily tires • Frequent illnesses • Enjoys out of doors; gym	• Likes to "work" • Likes to explain things • Quick to explain things • Show & tell is useful • Loves jokes & guessing games • Boisterous & enthusiastic language • Worrier; complainer • Anticipates closure in speech of others	• Wants to be first • Competitive; enthusiastic • Anxious to do well • Thrives on praise • Any failure is hard • Tremendous capacity for enjoyment • Likes surprises, treats • Wants to be good in school • Tends to be "poor sport" • Invents rules • Can be bossy, teasing • Critical of others • Easily upset when hurt • Sometimes dishonest • Friends are important (may have a best friend) • Transitions are difficult • School replaces home as most significant environmental influence	• Loves to ask questions • Likes new games; ideas • Loves to color; paint • Learns best through discovery • Enjoys process more than product • Tries more than can accomplish (eyes bigger than stomach) • Dramatic play elaborated • Cooperative play elaborated • Representative symbols more important • Spatial relationships & functional relationships better understood • Beginning understanding of *past* when tied closely to present • Beginning interest in skill & technique for its own sake

THE SIX YEAR OLD—CLASSROOM IMPLICATIONS

Six is the stage of "sorting out," of great drive and eagerness. There are many important classroom considerations.

Vision and Fine Motor Ability	• Children should do little copy work from the blackboard. While they will comply if asked, this is a difficult task at this age. • Spacing and the ability to stay on the line are difficult and performed with great inconsistency. • Tracking ability now makes reading instruction manageable.
Gross Motor Ability	• Teacher needs to allow for a busy level of noise and activity in the classroom. • Teacher should expect high volume of products but low quality of completion. Children are proud of how much work they get done, but not too concerned with how it looks. • Teachers can sometimes encourage a slower pace to enhance quality. • Teachers should pay attention to how much children delight in the doing; especially the doing for themselves, whether it be academics, clean-up or snack. Children are ready for experiments with individual and group responsibility.
Cognitive Growth	• Games of all sorts are popular and useful at this age. Language games, poems, riddles, and songs delight and illuminate the young mind. Teaching through games produces learning patterns that take root in a way that workbook learning usually does not. • This is an age of artistic explosion. Clay, paints, coloring, book making, weaving, dancing, singing are often all tried out for the first time with seriousness at this age. Children need to be made to feel that their attempts are valued, that there is a right and wrong way to approach an art medium. Risk taking at this age enhances later artistic expression and competence. • Children can begin to understand past events (history) when they are closely associated with the present. Teachers need to plan Social Studies content with an eye to the here and now. Field trips are immensely popular and productive when followed by representational activities such as experience stories and work in the blocks.
Personal-Social Behavior	• Extreme behavior needs to be understood but not excessively tolerated by the teacher. Tantrums, teasing, bossing, complaining, tattling are all ways sixes try out relationships with authority. • Teachers need to be extremely sensitive of the power of their words with children at this age. An ounce of praise may be all a child needs to get over a difficult situation; severe criticism can truly injure. • Teachers need to be aware to take the competitive edge off games as they employ them for learning. Sixes are highly competitive and can overdo the need to win and be first.

The Seven Year Old

"Nobody likes me, everybody hates me; think I'll go and eat some worms."

— Children's song

The familiar playground song must have been composed by a seven year old. It is the way they often feel. At seven children become extremely self-absorbed and self-conscious in their behavior. They are often moody, sulking, depressed. They spend long periods in their rooms, alone of their own choice, reading or listening to records or playing with animals or dolls. At school they like to work by themselves and appreciate quiet corners for reading or working. They may have a best friend, but relationships can be very on and off.

This is an inwardized, consolidated period of growth. Visually, children are myopic and concentrate on the details in their visual field. Note well their tiny printing and drawing; their pincer grip down on the lead of their pencils; their heads down on their arms or desks as they write, sometimes with one eye closed. Because of their visual concentration, sevens have great difficulty copying from the board and should be given little of this task. Physically, sevens now have a good working concept of right and left and general directionality.

Sevens are hard workers and often

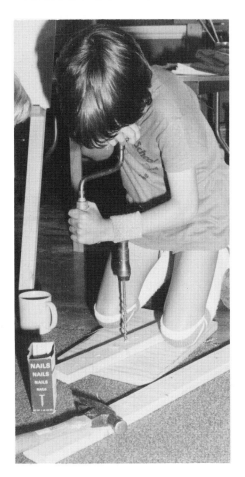

perfectionists. Where sixes are fond of the pencil sharpener, sevens adore the eraser. If they make mistakes they will erase and erase, sometimes putting a hole right through the paper. They want to be correct and they want their work to look good, too. Because of this tendency they take a long time with everything they do and become very upset when they are not given time to finish their work. Timed tests can be extremely upsetting at this age. Sevens love the routine and structure of school and appreciate their personal relationship with the teacher. Substitute teachers often have a frustrating time with sevens because they are constantly being told "that's not the way Teacher does it!"

In the classroom, sevens are good listeners and still enjoy being read a story. They show great interest in new words, number relationships and codes. They like working and talking with one other person, but do not do well on group projects. Board games (played with one other person) are a favorite.

At six children are noisy, verbal, active and brash; at seven, quiet, specific, passive and tense. Sevens' industriousness is now concentrated on individual work. Sevens hone in on what they can do and practice it over and over. If someone copies their work, the seven year old becomes extremely upset. Music lessons, often introduced at this age, can be both rewarding and frustrating.

"I quit!" is often heard both at home and on the playground; it is not because they did not get their own way (though we often interpret it this way), but because of an overwhelming feeling of inferiority that they may walk away from a group game or family project. Sevens' feelings need to be protected. Teasing, joking and especially sarcasm is painful to the seven year old. Being laughed at for a wrong answer or a "silly" idea produces anger and tears. Where these feelings were responded to with a punch at six, seven year olds drive these feelings deep inside and are less apt to risk themselves the next time they are called on or asked to do something.

Seven is an age where the child is driven by curiosity and the strong internal desire to discover and invent. As they consolidate logical thinking, they begin to organize their internal mental structures in new ways. Now they can classify spontaneously for the first time. (Black bear, brown bear, grizzly bear, koala bear! they chant excitedly). They are intensely interested in how things work and love to take things apart and put them back together again if they can.

Working in a block corner holds as much fascination for the seven as for children at younger ages. LEGO® blocks and other small manipulatives are favorites.

Sevens are beginning to deal with concepts of time, space and quantity with increased sophistication. While they still must act on their environment in order to understand it, they are increasingly able to represent their understanding symbolically in writing and drawing. Writing can be a favorite activity when children are given extended periods to create their own stories and narratives.

Science and Social Studies take on new meaning as sevens show increasing interest in the world around them. This interest will continue to expand and differentiate through ages eight, nine and ten. It is therefore, important to introduce global concepts slowly and with an eye toward sequential understanding. (The child's city or town is best studied and understood before using textbooks to examine desert or mountain villages in foreign countries!)

The child's increasing ability to utilize abstract reasoning, to infer, predict and estimate makes mathematical concepts particularly accessible at this age as long as the child continues to be given concrete manipulatives to work out these concepts before they are transferred to numeric abstractions.

Seven is an age of intensity. Individualized activity consolidates new internal structures and feelings. A balance between industry and inferiority produces a sense of competence, setting the stage for greater self-direction at older ages.

THE SEVEN YEAR OLD—BEHAVIORAL CHARACTERISTICS

PHYSICAL	LANGUAGE	PERSONAL-SOCIAL	ADAPTIVE
• Visually myopic • Works with head down on desk • Pincer grasp at pencil point • Written work tidy and neat • Sometimes tense • Likes confined space	• Good listener • Precise talker • Likes one-to-one conversation • Vocabulary development expands rapidly • Interested in meaning of words • Likes to send notes • Interested in all sorts of codes	• Inwardized, withdrawn • Sometimes moody; depressed; sulking or shy • Touchy • "Nobody likes me" • Changeable feelings • Needs security, structure • Relies on teacher for help • Doesn't like to make mistakes or risk making them • Sensitive to others' feelings, but sometimes tattles • Conscientious; serious • Keeps a neat desk, room • Needs constant reinforcement • Doesn't relate well to more than one teacher • Strong likes and dislikes	• Likes to review learning • Needs closure; must complete assignments • Likes to work slowly • Likes to work alone • Can classify spontaneously • Likes to be read to • Reflective ability growing • Erases constantly, wants work perfect • Likes to repeat tasks • Likes board games • Enjoys manipulatives • Wants to discover how things work; likes to take things apart

THE SEVEN YEAR OLD—CLASSROOM IMPLICATIONS

Sevens are "inwardized," moody; like to work alone. The classroom teacher needs to be alert to this sensitive age.

Vision and Fine Motor Ability	• Children's printing, drawing, number work tends to be small, if not microscopic. Children work with head down on desk, often hiding or closing one eye. Copying from the board can be harmful. Inappropriate time to introduce cursive handwriting. • Children will anchor printing to bottom line; find it difficult to fill up space. • Children work with pincer grasp at pencil point and find it difficult to relax their grip.
Gross Motor Level	• Teachers can plan for quiet room, sustained, quiet work periods with little overflow behavior. • Children prefer board games to gym games. Playground games such as jump rope, 4 square, hopscotch become more popular than team or large group activities.
Cognitive Growth	• Teachers need to pay special attention to routine and the child's need for closure. Children want to finish the work they begin. Timed tests can be especially troublesome. • Children like to work by themselves or in two's. Memorization is a favored pursuit. Children enjoy codes, puzzles and other secrets. • Children want their work to be perfect. Classroom attention to products, proper display of work, is entirely appropriate. • Children enjoy repeating tasks, reviewing assignments verbally with the teacher; like to touch base frequently with the teacher. • Teachers can successfully employ "discovery" centers or projects; children are dying to find out how things work. Like to collect and classify.
Personal-Social Behavior	• Teachers should expect frequent friendship shifts. Children work best in pairs or alone; will accept teacher seating assignments. • Change in schedule is upsetting; plan well for substitutes. • Teachers need to modulate seriousness of classroom for sevens with humor and games. • Communication with parents often critical during this changeable age.

DEVELOPMENTAL CONSIDERATIONS IN THE ELEMENTARY GRADES

Educators who are conversant with developmental theory will find the following chart of interest. The theories of Gesell, Piaget and Erikson are placed side by side to provide one example of a cross-age reference. Maturational, cognitive and psycho-social forces are considered between the ages of 4 and 12. Comparing developmental theories at given ages often is helpful in pinpointing specific behaviors and identifying useful classroom strategies.

DEVELOPMENTAL CONSIDERATIONS IN THE ELEMENTARY GRADES

AGE	GESELL (maturational)	PIAGET (cognitive)	ERIKSON (psychosocial)
4	**EXPANSION...** • Visually on the horizon • Expansive language • Out-of-bounds behavior	**PREOPERATIONAL...** • Child bound by what child sees • Cannot yet think logically • Egocentric (rules) • Uses intuitive thought • Animistic • Literal • Centered • Importance of play • Learning through discovery • Least like adults	**INITIATIVE VS. GUILT** • Conflicts between new energy of independence and limits of self and society • Visions of independent accomplishments not consistent with child's size and skills • Inability to achieve independent visions and act within boundaries creates internalized guilt • Environmental influences: parents, family, friends help set societal limits
4½	**FITTING TOGETHER...** • Opposition, inconsistency • Is it real? • Nightmares, short attention span		
5	**SMOOTH...** • Focal, centered, "good" • Literal, self-limiting • Adults can do no wrong		
5½	**BREAK-UP...** • Quick mood changes; peaks & valleys • Visual & Auditory disorganization • Dawdling		**RESOLUTION:** **A SENSE OF PURPOSE** • Child limits own visions and behavior without giving up ambition and and initiative
6	**SORTING OUT...** • Like to be first • Action oriented • Difficult transitions • Good ocular pursuit		
7	**INWARDIZED...** • Good listeners • Moody, depressed, quiet • Take time with work, thoughtful	**CONCRETE OPERATIONS...** • Mental action; the beginning of logical thought • Reversibility • Conservation • Seriation • Classification • Cooperation (rules)	**INDUSTRY VS. INFERIORITY** • Conflicts between desire to learn skills and fears of inadequacy • Child wants to develop self in socially-accepted ways • Learns to work and play with peers • Environmental influence: school
8	**EXPANSION...** • Exaggerate • Peer oriented		
9	**FITTING TOGETHER...** • Competitive • Accept responsibility • Truthful; individualistic		**RESOLUTION:** **SENSE OF COMPETENCE** • Growing confidence in abilities
10	**SMOOTH...** • Productive • Cooperative		
11	**BREAK-UP...** • Cliques, friendship shifts, loyalties • Moody	**FORMAL OPERATIONS...** • Ability to abstract • Deductive reasoning • Decentering • Codification (rules)	**IDENTITY VS. ROLE CONFUSION** • Conflict between growth into adulthood and confusing adolescent and adult roles • Environmental influence: peers
12	**SORTING OUT...** • Action oriented • Peer dominated		**RESOLUTION:** **FIDELITY TO OTHERS AND NEW, ADULT IDENTITY**

Comparative Work of Children

BUILDING WITH BLOCKS

The child's changing view of the world, together with visual and motor development produce observable patterns in block construction in the classroom.

Five-Six year old

Seven year old

Comparative Work of Children

BODY POSTURE

Simple observations of children's work postures can give clue to developmental age. For instance, 5 year olds fall out of their chairs sideways; six year olds, backwards.

FIVE YEAR OLD

The five year old shows ocular fixation, attending to one detail at a time. Posture is steady.

FIVE AND A HALF YEAR OLD

At five and a half there is more visual confusion, body shifts. The non-dominant hand tracks across the page, following the dominant hand.

SIX YEAR OLD

The six year old has good ocular pursuit and can track visually across the page left to right and back right to left.

SEVEN YEAR OLD

The seven year old is visually myopic. Posture often finds the head close to the paper; fingers close to pencil point. Printing becomes tiny, copying from the board a near impossibility.

Comparative Work of Children

THE DEVELOPMENTAL EXAMINATION
(Paper and Pencil Subtest)

Children are asked to write their names, the numbers that they
know and to copy standardized geometric forms.

Five year old

Five and a half year old

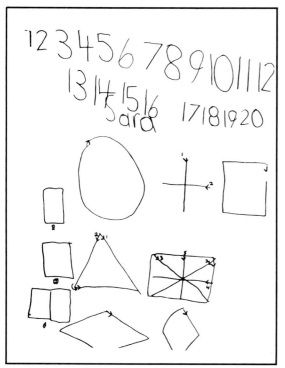

Six year old

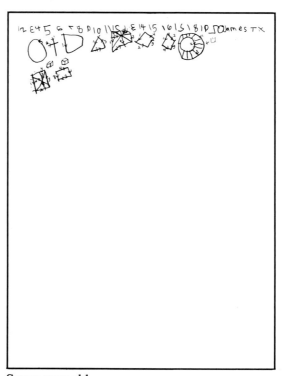

Seven year old

COMPARATIVE RESPONSES OF CHILDREN

Children's responses to Gesell School Readiness Test show variations
in development levels. Note reversals of typical 5½ year old, small size
of work at 7, large size at 6. Note completion of triangle at 5, 6 and 7.
General organization of child's work shows differing adaptive abilities.

Comparative Work of Children

VISUAL DEVELOPMENT AND MOTOR CO-ORDINATION

Visual developmental and motor co-ordination dictate a progressive but nonlinear growth pattern. Adult-like ability is the final goal, but will not be attained until 10 to 12 years of age.

Seven year old

Five year old

Six year old

A PRACTICAL APPROACH

- Developmental Curriculum: A Definition
- The Classroom Environment
- What to Teach
- The Planning Process

Developmental Curriculum: A Definition

A developmental curriculum is carefully framed on knowledge about children's physical, social and intellectual growth. It is based on what children need to learn and what we know about how they learn. Teachers adjust the curriculum through their understanding of each child and the group of children.

What does a developmental curriculum look like when it is implemented?

- Children have time during the day to explore their environment.

- The teacher and environment provide opportunities for children to experiment, solve problems, and make fruitful mistakes.

- Teachers use an inquiry approach, asking thoughful, intelligent questions which may have several right answers.

- Children make choices about learning each day.

- Teachers pay careful attention to how children treat each other and reinforce respect as the basis for interaction.

- Children's ideas, creations, and discoveries are valued and displayed around the room.

- Teachers spend a part of each day observing children at work.

- The room is a home where children can learn through cooking as well as writing, woodworking as well as social studies, and where they can explore feelings, dreams and conflicts.

- Children's work is measured and evaluated against developmental milestones.

The specific learning approaches used in our curriculum are chosen because they are consistent with the principles of developmental education. Many have been introduced by Bank Street College of Education, Educational Development Center, High Scope, and other staff development centers. Effective approaches include:

- Language experience
- Math manipulatives
- Block building
- Inventive spelling
- Classroom meetings
- Discovery approach
- Cross-age tutoring.

A Balanced Approach

The child and the content find their proper place when teachers use scientific knowledge of normative growth patterns. The learning environment balances school expectations with the child's developmental level.

Child-Initiated Learning

The content is lost when children dictate the curriculum in the name of open education. Lack of professional direction and structure limits growth and produces unnecessary failure.

Teacher-Directed Learning

The child's needs and abilities are lost when the teacher emphasizes intellectual achievement and early skill acquisition, and directs all learning activity in the classroom.

The Classroom
Environment

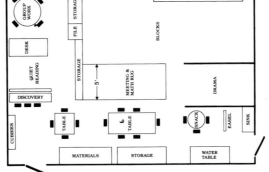

The classroom pictured in the following photo-essay is a combination kindergarten-first grade at the Greenfield Center School. The Greenfield Center School, located in Western Massachusetts, is the laboratory school of the Northeast Foundation for Children. It is a school that is dedicated to building a developmental curriculum that balances what we know about children with what children want and need to know. This essay illustrates one way to implement a developmental curriculum. It is a model that works.

FLOOR PLAN

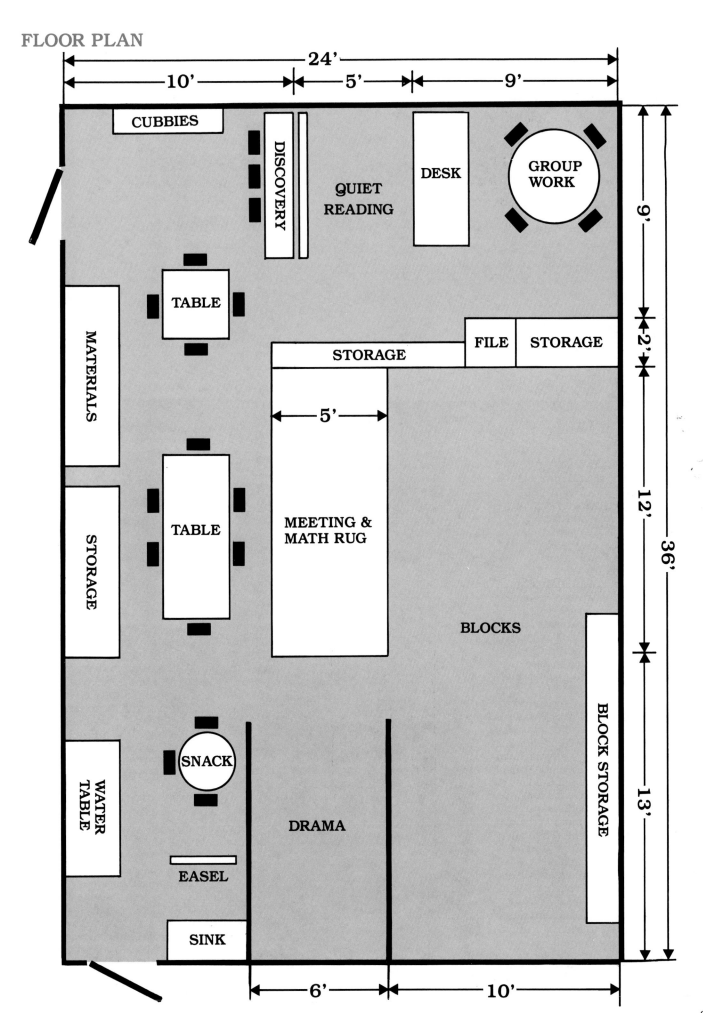

The Classroom

In the classroom, children begin their days by working on their plans. Ms. Clayton is completing her "News and Announcements" chart for the day.

A developmental classroom can be read again and again. Its arrangement and contents have a language and a meaning. The Greenfield Center School's primary classroom, a combination kindergarten-first grade (for developmental five and six year olds) which unfolds over the next few pages, is a rich, vibrant, and comfortable place.

Its corners are alive with places to write, to build, to play house, to do puzzles, to snack, to paint, to read, to drift off into a private world. It is a room which says that children's ideas, accomplishments and creations are important, that there are things to discover, new skills to learn, and enough time to take risks and make mistakes in learning.

In order to create such a room, the teacher, Marlynn Clayton, is involved in an on-going process of skillful planning, organizing, collecting, researching, inventing, observing, revising and refining.

The Greenfield
Center School—a
traditional exterior
masks the warmth
and diversity
within.

Ms. Clayton works with two of her
students in writing. She is telling
Erin, "Write the sounds that you hear."

Art Space

The shelves, the areas laden with equipment and materials, are carefully labeled and organized. Each material and tool has a specific place which is labeled with words and pictures. When a project is finished children return everything where it belongs.

The teacher provides places to display and hang children's projects. The room overflows with the creations of the children. There are "show shelves" for three dimensional clay, woodworking, LEGO® blocks or TINKERTOY® building set projects. Children make signs for the displays.

Blocks

Blocks and drama corner are active, noisy areas taking up the largest amount of space.

In the block area, people, cars, furniture and found materials motivate the fives and sixes to build things in the here-and-now-houses, restaurants and places that they know.

Once a building is done, what happens? Does it just stand there? It can be looked at, but it also needs to have a use. The children discuss different ways to use their buildings.

The blocks are taken down, not knocked down. They are stacked in certain numbers, and once the building is taken apart, the stacks of blocks are moved over to the shelf and put away. Every block has its own place. The children have a sense of organization and care.

Discovery

The discovery table is placed near the light since animals and plants will be growing there.

Drama

In the drama corner language and writing experiences continue.

Independence, self-control and responsibility are fostered in an environment in which the children have access to materials, a part in planning, problems to solve, choices and decisions to make.

Reading

The library area is cozy, quiet, inviting.

The room provides an area for children to work on manipulatives: puzzles, CUISENAIRE® rods, LEGO® blocks. Cooking is math, sorting is math, woodworking is math, building is math. Math is concrete in the room.

Materials, tools and some new ideas are provided, but they are such that the children can use them to create experiences for themselves. Ms. Clayton does not make something for them. The children take what is put out and explore, experiment and produce from within themselves. As they work, Ms. Clayton observes and questions, learning what the children understand about their work and where they need to go next.

Management

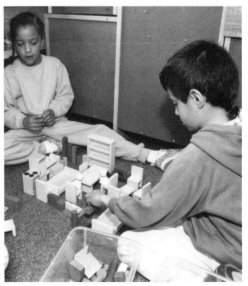

School Rule

Treat other people just like you want to be treated back.

There are rules about classroom behavior, care of the room and care of each other in the room. The rules are written down, put up on a chart where all can refer to them as needed. Ms. Clayton talks about the care of each area, what happens in each area and how many people can be there.

Children can move freely from one area to another without distracting others. During the year as the children grow, their needs change and the room changes.

Low dividers define activity areas, allowing easy observation of children at work, and letting children know that they can be seen. In such an environment children feel safe and free to work independently.

Areas are labeled in words and pictures so that children know how many can work to-gether in a particular area.

Fives and sixes are gregarious and the way that they learn is by working together. They love to play games. They love to work together, to build together. They try out taking turns, winning, losing, following rules. They learn from each other, learn to listen, to share ideas and materials.

Outdoor Play

Outside the classroom the fives and sixes continue to develop their understanding of how to play and work with one another.

"What supplies should I have in my classroom for five and six year olds?"

The following list includes two categories for each interest area in the classroom: 1) **equipment**—which refers to purchased items that remain in the class over a long perod of time, and 2) **supplies**—which refers to items bought or found that are to be used and replaced.

BLOCK AREA
Equipment:
- [ ] unit blocks—many sizes and shapes and enough for a whole class to build if possible
- [ ] small blocks (plain, not colored)
- [ ] wooden furniture
- [ ] people figurines—families, community workers
- [ ] animals—farm and zoo
- [ ] cars, trucks, tractors, buses, airplanes
- [ ] LEGO® blocks
- [ ] pulleys

Supplies:
- [ ] PLASTICINE® modeling material
- [ ] wire
- [ ] string
- [ ] found materials like shells, buttons, scraps of material, cardboard tubes, seeds, sticks, etc.
- [ ] pipe cleaners
- [ ] paper
- [ ] markers

Blocks Area—Outside:
- [ ] large hollow wooden blocks, wood planks, steering wheels, tires

DRAMA CORNER
Equipment:
- [ ] stove
- [ ] sink
- [ ] refrigerator
- [ ] doll bed
- [ ] dress-ups
- [ ] puppets
- [ ] curtain
- [ ] bean bags
- [ ] NERF® balls
- [ ] VELCRO® darts and board
- [ ] tables and chairs
- [ ] pots and pans
- [ ] utensils and dishes
- [ ] mirror
- [ ] dolls
- [ ] empty food cans, boxes, cartons
- [ ] props for school, doctor's office
- [ ] props for fire dept., groceries
- [ ] indoor basketball hoop

Supplies:
- [ ] paper
- [ ] clay
- [ ] small blackboards
- [ ] crayons
- [ ] markers
- [ ] pencils
- [ ] chalk
- [ ] cardboard

GAME LOFT
Equipment: (these are *not* all made available at same time)
- [ ] CONNECT FOUR® game
- [ ] checkers
- [ ] CHUTES AND LADDERS® game
- [ ] Chinese checkers
- [ ] CANDY LAND® game
- [ ] dominoes
- [ ] handmade games
- [ ] attribute block and people pieces games
- [ ] several decks of cards with large numbers
- [ ] SORRY® game
- [ ] UNO® game
- [ ] HO-HO-CHERRY-O® game
- [ ] MANCALA® game
- [ ] LOTTO® cards
- [ ] bingo

Supplies: (available so that children can make games)
- [ ] old game board
- [ ] cardboard
- [ ] dice
- [ ] index cards
- [ ] buttons
- [ ] old game markers
- [ ] spinners

SAND-WATER TABLE
Equipment:
- [ ] a solid table with good quality liner that has a drain
- [ ] a variety of sizes and shapes of spoons, cups, dishes, bottles, cans, and pans
- [ ] sponges, buckets, plastic tubing, pumps

Supplies:
- [ ] clean fine sand
- [ ] dried beans
- [ ] split peas—orange are attractive
- [ ] found materials—shells, rocks, seeds, sticks, corks, styrofoam, etc.

LIBRARY AND LISTENING CENTER
Equipment:
- [ ] variety of books including picture books with no words, easy picture books, easy readers, harder books of familiar stories or poems that have been read to the class like *Charlotte's Web, Mother Goose* or Shel Silverstein's *Where the Sidewalk Ends*, magazines like Ranger Rick, children's individual published books, class experience books.
- [ ] 2 or 3 books a week on tape from library list that children may listen to as they look at book.

ART
Equipment:
- [ ] painting easel
- [ ] peg board for drying
- [ ] shelves for drying, storage and display
- [ ] stamps
- [ ] scissors
- [ ] brayers
- [ ] variety of brushes
- [ ] smocks
- [ ] stencils
- [ ] hole punches
- [ ] printing plates

Supplies
- [ ] markers
- [ ] CRAY-PAS® colors
- [ ] PAYONS® crayons
- [ ] variety of pencils
- [ ] clay
- [ ] ink
- [ ] variety of tapes
- [ ] candles
- [ ] string
- [ ] material
- [ ] buttons
- [ ] found materials from nature and from industry (boxes, wire, newspaper, Q-TIPS® cotton swabs, straw, cotton, old toothbrushes)
- [ ] crayons
- [ ] colored pencils
- [ ] watercolors
- [ ] pipe cleaners
- [ ] PLASTICINE® modeling material
- [ ] rulers
- [ ] pastels
- [ ] yarn
- [ ] thread
- [ ] wood pieces

MATH AND MANIPULATION AREA
Equipment:
- [ ] CUISENAIRE® rods
- [ ] attribute blocks
- [ ] number balance
- [ ] handmade games
- [ ] UNIFIX® cubes
- [ ] playing cards

DISCOVERY TABLE
Equipment:
- [ ] aquariums
- [ ] microscope
- [ ] mirrors
- [ ] various containers to hold living and nonliving
- [ ] materials, containers to grow plants in
- [ ] magnifying glasses
- [ ] magnets
- [ ] balances

What to Teach

A developmental curriculum is a program of study, skill acquisition and achievement sequenced in specific relationship to children's cognitive and socio-emotional growth patterns. Such a curriculum does not ignore the scope and sequence and content of standard instruction. It utilizes this content fully by introducing it to children when they are ready for it and in a way that makes them responsible for being able to use it.

As teachers we expect children to master the basic skill of reading; however, we should not anticipate that this skill be acquired by all children at the same age or in the same way. Further, we expect children to have basic skills in mathematical computation, spelling, composition and expression, but they should not be expected to do so at uniform times or grades.

These skills *are* acquired in a natural sequence that the skilled teacher manages. Through formed methods and systematic instruction students learn their basic skills. In a developmental classroom, a planned environment allows students to learn to make choices, initiate and pursue tasks, solve problems, communicate and demonstrate a responsible investment in their own learning.

It is *because* of the dynamic, interactive approach to curriculum and teaching that we cannot offer a step-by-step guide to teachers. A developmental curriculum and a step-by-step guide are diametrically opposed. We can, however, offer a closer look at several curriculum areas, discussing approach and rationale, giving some suggestions for activities and sharing resources and materials that we have found invaluable in implementing a developmental curriculum.

Ultimately a developmental curriculum is an on-going process in a carefully planned environment that reflects the needs and interests of a group of children and their teacher.

Reading and Writing for the Five to Seven Year Old

Children are highly social beings who have a strong desire to think, learn, and communicate about their lives. Our approach to reading and writing builds upon this motivation. We provide a program that emphasizes language experience, process writing (see Graves, Calkins pp. 70-71), and a literature-based approach to reading instruction. Children see their own language in print. They enjoy well-respected literature of all genres and cultures. They move their bodies to rhymes, chants, songs and dramatizations. They employ a variety of language learning strategies; they predict and confirm based on their growing use of illustrations, semantics, syntax, phonics, word configurations and other textual cues. By asking young children to write about their own experiences in whatever way they can, free of spelling, grammar or handwriting rules, we foster the desire to read and write. Older children will learn these rules and are directed to apply their skills to record events, explore interests and queries using a rich supply of texts and source materials, including people from the community, films, audio and video tapes, magazines and newspapers. Children learn to read through their writing and to write through their reading. We believe the two skills are integrally connected.

As we examine a few specifics of each age level it is critical to remember that we are committed to the concept of a developmental progression rather than strict age/grade markers. Therefore, as we speak of our approach to reading and writing with the five year old, for example, we are also including a certain portion of the six-year-old population.

Five year olds are ready for reading and writing but not for reading and writing instruction as traditionally taught. Given what we understand about children's reading/writing development and motivation to learn, programs based on controlled language texts, meaningless workbook exercises and endless handwriting drills are inappropriate and ineffective. We give the five year old a language- and experience-rich environment where music, stories, plays and ther own language provide the foundation—"the storehouse"—for their growing mastery of reading and writing. Five year olds need to draw, paint, build and sculpt to tell, or rehearse their stories. They can then comfortably write their stories by forming the letters of the sounds they hear in words. Reading and writing come from "the storehouse" of language including sounds, symbols and ideas.

The six and seven year old is reaching the Piagetian stage of concrete operational thinking and is thus ready for more formal instruction in reading and writing. We provide formal instruction for reading based on content, interest, need, and learning style. Through whole group, small group, partner, and individual conference formats, we continue to build and enrich "the storehouse" of language. As six and seven year olds become more fluent readers, they are ready to incorporate more standard spelling and grammar into their own writing. Each child in her/his individual work shows the teacher what has been mastered and what instructional steps need to follow.

Reading/Writing Activities for the Five to Seven Year Old

- label classroom work areas
- write class rules in children's language (state positively) and post at children's eye level
- write daily chart including day, date, weather, information about activities, jobs and special events using both predictable and less familiar language; play word games with the chart involving naming, matching, recognizing, rhyming, revising, and writing words, phrases, letters, sounds and letter clusters
- write children's news on chart (sevens can record their own news)
- children take turns choosing a word for the day from their own experi-

rABOS
r
FAGT L

Rainbows are fragile.

ence or interests; the word goes onto the class word ring, is used in sentences and word games (see daily chart activity)

- children write daily snack menu or lunch menu
- create charts with favorite poems, rhymes, chants, songs, and stories that use predictable language; read together; play word games (see daily chart activity); put in music, dramatize, collect into class poem or song books; create books with an individual poem, song, story, or illustration; write separate charts leaving certain words blank and let children revise using their own words, make individual books of children's revised poems, songs and stories

EXAMPLE:

1 2 3 4 5, I caught a_____alive.
6 7 8 9 10, I let him/her/it go again.

- write group poems together, post as charts, play word games with them (see daily chart activity), put in book form, illustrate, dramatize
- teacher reads picture or chapter books aloud on a daily basis
- children select literature to be read individually, with partners, or in small groups; teach conferences with children focusing on comprehension, oral reading and skill development; children choose from a range of follow-up activities
- children label block buildings, paintings and drawings, clay, and LEGO® block constructions in their own writing
- write simple directions for games and art or science projects with words and pictures (sixes and sevens can create their own games, art and science projects and write directions)
- write a favorite recipe on a chart, read it, cook from it, play word games with it (see daily chart activity), write children's comments about it, collect several into book form, illustrate
- write stories about field trips, class events or children in the class using children's words (everyone contributes); read, use for word games (see daily chart activity), make into a class book, dramatize, use as a copying (handwriting) exercise for sixes and sevens
- children write their own non-fiction stories and reports about school-based events and field trips, read them to the group, make them into a newspaper or class book, share with other classes

- children write their own stories or poems in rough draft; teacher and children conference, revise, and edit; teacher or parents type edited copy making additional corrections for spelling and punctuation; children illustrate and bind into a book; book goes into class library and is used as instructional reading material
- record books onto tape for children to use in a listening center; children may record their own published books as well
- write plays with children, dramatize, write in book form for others to read and use (sevens can write up their own plays)
- children write and read their daily plans
- children write weekly reports of one or two school experiences to be taken home and shared (fives and sixes need to do it more with illustrations)
- children write about math, science, water, sand, and art discoveries to be shared and then verified by others

EXAMPLE:

One child writes after working with these materials:
"Wet sand is heavier than dry sand."
Then other children write about how they proved or disproved this hypothesis.

Curriculum Materials Useful for Implementing the Developmental Approach in Reading and Writing

(Also see RESOURCES: Bibliography under "Reading, Writing, Spelling")

1. *Bill Martin's Instant Readers.* Bill Martin Jr. and Peggy Brogan. New York: Holt Rhinehart and Winston, Inc., 1971.
2. *The Griffin Pirate Stories.* Sheila K. McCullagh. Elmsford, NY: Pergamon Press, Inc., 1970. Revised.

3. *Ladybird Books.* Available through Ladybird Books, 19 Omni Circle, Auburn, ME.
4. Children's literature appropriate for use with reading groups:

- *American Folksongs for Children.* Ruth Seeger. New York: Doubleday, 1948.
- Dell Yearling Books, Dell Young Yearling Books, and Dell Yearling Classics (various authors). New York: Dell Publishing Co.
- "I Can Read" Books (various authors) New York: Harper & Row.
- *The Random House Book of Poetry for Children.* Jack Prelutsky (Ed.). New York: Random House, 1983.
- "Ready-to-Read" Books (various authors). New York: Macmillan.
- Rigby Books (various authors). Crystal Lake, IL: Rigby.
- Scholastic Books (various authors). Jefferson City, MO: Scholastic.
- "Sounds of Language" Series. Bill Martin, Jr. with Peggy Brogan & John Archaumbault. Allen, TX: DLM, 1990.
- Sundance (various authors). Littleton, MA: Sundance.
- Troll Books (various authors). Mahway, NJ: Troll Assoc.
- *Words I Use When I Write.* Alana Trisler and Patrice Howe Cardiel. Montrose NJ: Modern Learning Press/Programs for Education. (also *More Words I Use When I Write*).
- The Wright Group (various authors). San Diego, CA: The Wright Group.

Mathematics for the Five to Seven Year Old

It is our belief that in order to achieve math literacy and computational competence, children must begin with immersion in mathematical concepts that play a role in their everyday lives. The manipulation of objects and the use of materials in the environment leads to problem solving which is real and useful to children. Math activities grounded in children's experience enhance interest in the solution, increase attention to the details of mathematical approaches, and lead to the generalization of concepts and procedures. The learning and mastery of mathematical concepts does not come from the completion of workbook pages. Children use workbooks only to practice concepts already mastered using concrete objects and real-life problem solving experiences.

Again, we do not have a step-by-step developmental math curriculum guide. It is each teacher's job to observe children based on knowledge of mathematical development (for example, see sample report page 56) and introduce needed skills and concepts through an active exploration and manipulation of materials. We do have a list of concrete activities and published resources and materials that we have found to be extremely useful.

Concrete Math Activities for the Five to Seven Year Old

- use group surveys about class characteristics and interests to explore concepts in counting, computation, sorting and classifying
  — with fives and sixes use real objects or drawings of objects to graph; verbally discuss graph with group; than ask challenge questions to be answered by individuals or partners throughout the week
  — with six and one half and sevens, allow them to carry out surveys individually; sevens can begin to interpret graphs on their own and do written follow-up activities
- use games to teach many math concepts: board games, card games, active physical games, dramatization games (restaurant, store), memory games; use materials that are of interest to children
  — children show mastery in the way they teach a game to another child
  — children show mastery in their ability to make up their own games
- use the daily schedule to play games and ask questions about time, make time books about the daily schedule and about children's lives away from school

- create daily math rituals based on daily chart information (days of the week, date, weather, number of days of school, money, attendance) that teach counting, patterning, sequencing, graphing, computation, place value
- use constructions in the block area for activities in counting, estimation, fractions, geometry, measurement, computation, sorting and classifying
- use the snack and lunch menu for problems in computation, counting, fractions, measurements, sorting and classifying
- invent a daily or weekly "Mystery Problem" involving children and events in class
- use cooking for activities in time, measurement, estimation, computation, fractions, balance
- use field trips to explore concepts in time, measurement, mapping, money computation, sorting and classifying
- use the water-sand table for activities that explore concepts in balance, measurement, estimation, one-to-one correspondence, comparison, counting, volume, density
- use clean up and organization of room to explore concepts of sorting and classifying, patterns, estimation, time
- use music, movement, sewing, woodworking, painting, and art activities to explore concepts in patterning, sequence, symmetry, time, counting, measurement, computation, estimation, fractions, geometry

Curriculum Materials Useful for Implementing the Developmental Approach in Mathematics

(Also see RESOURCES: Bibliography under Mathematics)

1. Attribute Blocks®, Pattern Blocks® and related materials. Available through Creative Publications, Oak Lawn, IL or Palo Alto, CA.
2. CUISENAIRE® Rods, Materials and Instruction Books. New Rochelle, NY: Cuisenaire Co. of America.
3. *Elementary Science Study.* Units in Measurement, Mapping. Attributes, Pattern Blocks, Balancing and Estimating. Available through Delta Education, Hudson, NH.
4. *Family Math.* Jean Kerr Stenmark, Virginia Thompson, Ruth Cossey. Berkeley, CA: Lawrence Hall of Science, University of California, 1986. Also available in Spanish.
5. LEGO® blocks. Enfield, CT: LEGO Dacta Educational Products.
6. *Mathematics.* C. Gattegno. New Rochelle, NY: Cuisenaire Co. of America.
7. *Mathematics Their Way.* Mary Baratta-Lorton. Reading, MA: Addison-Wesley Publishing, 1976.
8. *Saxon Math K-3.* Nancy Larson. Norman, OK: Saxon Publishers, 1991.
9. UNIFIX® cubes and materials; *Unifix Teacher's Manual.* Nixie Taverner. Available through Creative Publications, Oak Lawn IL or Palo Alto, CA.
10. *Workjobs.* Mary Baratta-Lorton. Reading, MA: Addison-Wesley Publishing, 1975.
11. *Workjobs II.* Mary Baratta-Lorton. Reading, MA: Addison-Wesley Publishing, 1979.
12. *Workjobs...for Parents.* Mary Baratta-Lorton. Reading, MA: Addison-Wesley Publishing, 1975.

Social Studies

We believe the purpose of a social studies curriculum is to bring children to an understanding of how their human world functions (e.g., how people get food and clothing, how people move about, what people do in their work, how people solve problems, etc.) and how the natural world functions (how plants and animals grow and affect each other, what makes and affects geography, how geography affects plants and animals, etc.) and how these two worlds affect each other. In our curriculum approach it is *not* the facts that children absorb about these worlds that is most important (though the facts *are* necessary). Rather, it is how children *use* the facts to discover new knowledge—the understanding of relationships in their world. We want children to build ways of seeing and thinking about the patterns and connections in their environment. Ultimately our goal is to help children learn to think and problem solve in a culture and world that is constantly changing.

"...it is only by explaining the 'here and now' that children grow in the capacity to discover relations— to think."
Lucy Sprague Mitchell

Children, five to seven years of age, are grounded in the "here and now"—in concrete experiences of their own environment. As we know, young children are at the center of their world, only able to see the world from their perspective and unable yet to understand concepts of time and space. They need a curriculum which will help them to see and discover relationships in their own world, not in a world of the past or the future. As they mature, they move away from their self-centered perspective and begin to struggle with concepts of time and space. It is this time, around 8 years of age, that children are ready to begin to look at other cultures and other times, but only in relation to what they understand about their own environment and time. Before this, children need to discover how their own environment functions and how the natural phenomena that they see, hear and feel in their everyday lives works. Children at this age come to these understandings through their own exploration and discovery. It is the dynamic creative process of their own discovery that builds relationship thinking.

Our social studies curriculum is two-fold in its approach and each part is critical to the educational process. First, we provide children with expe-riences and opportunities for observations in their immediate environment through many field trips. And second, in the classroom, we provide children with materials and methods through which they can experiment, discover, and express the information they're absorbing and the connections they're making about their trips and therefore their world. Let us look more closely at these two important components.

Field Trips

We do not have an itemized list of field trips that a five, six or seven year old should experience at each grade level. Every teacher must decide for herself what trips best suit the experiences, interests and age level of her students within the context of their environment, be it city, country or suburb. We do, however, have some developmental guidelines that teachers may use in thinking about appropriate trips and appropriate ways of looking at their environment for each age group, five to seven years of age. The curriculum does move on a continuum, ever broadening the range of study as the children developmentally move away from themselves as the center of their world. However, the basis of the curriculum remains the same—concrete experiences in the 'here and now'. Through the years of their growth, children will repeat trips but each trip offers new and richer experiences as the associations children bring to them deepen with their own maturation.

Five year olds are just coming to an understanding of the relationships of their home environment. They are ready to explore their home and family, their neighborhood (friend's homes, streets, parks, fields, etc.), their school and school yard (the classrooms, the cafeteria, the furnace room, the trees and plants, etc.) and the school's neighborhood (the nearby streets, shops, homes, buses, fields, factories, etc.). For example, a teacher might take a group of five year olds to investigate the school cafeteria. During their visit, they see where the food is kept and then prepared and served. These observations might lead to further studies of where the food comes from (a nearby store or dairy?), how food is delivered to the school, what are the jobs to be done in a cafeteria (and perhaps then a restaurant) or what are different ways food is preserved and what happens to food that is not. The five year old can see the realtionships that are closest to him in his immediate environment of home, neighborhood and school.

The six year old with more experience and understanding of his immediate environment is ready to explore a little further out into the community. He needs to follow the streets away from his school and home and discover what lies beyond. He's ready to look more closely at the businesses, the factories, the community services (water, waste, police, fire), the farms, the transportation, and the natural phenomena and forces (rain, rivers, mountains) that affect his community. For example, a teacher might take a group of six year olds to visit a market in their community where their school does its shopping. However, unlike the fives, who were following the route of only one or two food items from their school back to the store, the sixes are ready to explore the workings of the store as a whole. The six year old can discover relationships within each of these parts of his community and begin to struggle with their interrelationships.

It is the seven year old who can now look at the broader systems of his community. The systems still need to be ones that he can investigate concretely but he is ready to discover what makes a community, what a community needs to function and how each part is related and interconnected. For example, a seven year old might visit a supermarket in his community but unlike the fives and sixes, the visit would lead to much more than a study of the inner workings of the store. The sevens could be led to study the transportation in the community that services the store; the community services (electricity, water, waste) that help the store function, the community's media systems, the community's local food and goods suppliers, and the effects of natural forces on the workings of the store (weather, climate, geography). The avenues of study are almost without limit and each will lead to others, showing again in a concrete way the relationships that are there to be discovered and understood.

Field trips are the first component of our social studies curriculum. How the children are asked to express their experiences is the second component. Children, ages 5 to 7, learn best through constructive play where they can create what they have seen and act out what they have experienced. The materials and methods provided in the classroom are crucial to the kind of play that occurs. In order for children to make their own discoveries, they need materials and methods which are adaptable, varied and can show the thinking of the child. We have a list of some materials that we provide in our classrooms and some suggestions of ways a teacher can encourage children to use them. The materials and methods remain basically the same for children ages five to seven. What changes is the way the children *use* them to express what they're learning. Five-year-old expressions will be simple and more general. Gradually the play will become more detailed and complicated as children mature towards 7 and 8. Again, this list is only partial and is meant to be a guide.

Materials and Suggestions for Constructive Social Studies Play

BLOCKS (unit blocks—we believe to be one of the most important adaptable materials for children ages five to seven)

- build representations of what they've seen (house, store, farm, city block, school neighborhood)
- use to make 3-dimensional maps (school neighborhood, center of town, school)
- use to play out field experiences (how the store gets the bananas and milk, how different children get to school, how a restaurant operates, how boats dock and unload cargo)
- use constructions for group discussions about field trips

ART MATERIALS (clay, paints, wood, found materials, natural materials, yarn, crayons, cardboard)

- use to represent a part or all of what they've experienced
- use to supplement block structures and maps
- use to supplement drama materials

DRAMA MATERIALS (dress-ups, puppets, props)

- act out experiences through informal play in blocks, art or drama area
- act out experiences in formal way through skits, plays, scenes, puppet shows

SCIENCE MATERIALS (objects from nature found on trips or brought in by children, magnifying glasses, water-sand table, magnets, cages, balances, containers)

- use to observe (fives can share verbally or through art; sixes and sevens can *begin* to share through writing, too)
- use to experiment and play with (again best for fives to share results of play verbally, sixes and sevens *begin* to share results in other ways, too)
- use to represent a part, or all, of what they've experienced (e.g., the school yard in the sand table)

OTHER WAYS TO EXPRESS AND SHARE EXPERIENCES

- Bookmaking and tape recording
- Movement and dance
- Group discussions and experience charts
- Story telling individually or in a group

- Games (physical, board, verbal, sensory)
- Songs

A developmental approach to a social studies curriculum integrates all parts of the school curriculum. In both the field experiences and the classroom expression and discovery, children are developing and using their skill in reading, writing, language arts, mathematics, the arts, science and physical education.

Our approach is not new. It has been used for many years by teachers committed to a progressive and developmental point of view in education. There are a variety of resources that we have found valuable in carrying out our social studies and science curriculum. The following list and the Bibliography encompass many that are available.

Curriculum Materials Useful for Implementing the Developmental Approach in Social Studies and Science.

(Also see RESOURCES: Bibliography under Science and Social Studies)

1. Archiblocks® (architectural blocks). Available through ARCHIBLOCKS, Vergennes, VT.
2. *Doing What Scientists Do: Children Learn to Investigate Their World.* Ellen Doris. Portsmouth, NH: Heinemann Books and Northeast Foundation for Children, 1991. Available through Northeast Foundation for Children, Greenfield, MA.
3. *Elementary Science Study (ESS) Curriculum* (teachers' guides). Newton, MA: Educational Development Center. Available through Delta Education, Inc., Hudson, NH.
4. *Macdonald Science 5/13* (teachers' guides). Schools Council. London, England: Macdonald Educational Ltd., 1972. Available through Teacher's Laboratory, Brattleboro, VT.
5. Standard Unit Blocks and accessories (animals, furniture, people, cars). Available through Community Playthings, Rifton, NY.

6. *Teaching Primary Science* (teacher's guides). Chelsea College Project. Chelsea, England: 1976. Available through Teacher's Laboratory, Brattleboro, VT.
7. *Ten Minute Field Trips: Using the School Grounds for Environmental Studies.* Helen Ross Russell. Chicago: J.G. Ferguson Publishing Co., 1973
8. Trade books related to the field of study (about houses, bridges, snakes, rivers, etc.). Best bets:
   - Ladybird Series. Available through Ladybird Books, 19 Omni Circle, Auburn, ME.
   - Oxford Scientific Films books. Available through G.P. Putnam's Sons, New York.
   - Eyewitness Books. Available through Alfred A. Knopf, New York.
   - Practical Puffin Books. Available through Puffin Books, a division of Penguin Books, New York.
   - New True Books. Available through Children's Press, Chicago.
   - Usborne First Nature Books. Tulsa OK: EDC Publishing.
   - David Macaulay books (Unbuilding, Underground, Castle, Pyramid, The Way Things Work). Boston: Houghton Mifflin.

The Planning Process

The planning process is central to an effective developmental curriculum. Planning allows children to become active participants in their learning and allows teachers to foster the growing initiative in their students. Through the planning process, learning becomes a co-operative contract between teacher and child. Children begin to formulate the purposes which direct their learning and participate in the decisions and problem-solving necessary to execute the plan. Children learn responsibility and develop a positive independence in their approach to learning. The respectful "give and take" in the planning process builds valuable trust between teacher and child.

To formulate a plan each child must ask "What do I *want* to learn?" as well as "What do I *have* to learn?" The teacher's role is to guide the child in finding an appropriate balance of "have-to" (teacher-directed) and "choice" (child-initiated) activities. The teacher pays strict attention to the intentions of the plan and by suggestions and questions contributes to its construction. The extent and depth of planning follows a continuum based on age readiness. We start with the five year old who can be expected to plan one activity of the morning and then build gradually towards the 13 and 14 year old who can be expected to plan a week's activities and month-long projects.

Let us look more closely at the appropriate expectations for planning by children ages 5 to 7 and how a teacher might organize the process in his classroom.

PLANNING EXPECTATIONS

Five Year Olds
- need to hear about and discuss have-to's and choices daily before writing plan
- can complete one have-to requiring 15-20 minutes (usually in a small group)
- using a picture-cued plan sheet, can circle a have-to and plan one other activity for morning by copying words on sheet
- can be involved in many more activities then those planned

Six Year Olds
- need to hear about and discuss activities daily before writing plan
- can complete two have-to's in a morning—one requiring 15-20 minutes, one requiring 10-15 minutes
- using a picture and planning sheet, can circle have-to's and plan for 2 to 3 activities for the morning (possibly including have-to's) by copying words on sheet
- can be involved in many more activities than those planned

Seven Year Olds
- can write plans without daily verbal review of have-to's and choices
- can complete two have-to's requiring 20-30 minutes each in a day
- gradually moving into a nonpicture-cued plansheet, can plan three morning activities and one afternoon activity including have-to's by writing words
- will usually not be involved in more activities than those planned for in a morning

The key to the planning process for the teacher is careful organization. The organization must be consistent, making the teacher's expectations clear and the children's options known. It is the organization that allows the children to work responsibly, independently and, above all,

with success. In structuring a planning process for five to seven year olds, a teacher needs to include the following components:

- a daily sequential listing of groups to meet
- a daily listing of children's required work (have-to's)
- a consistent schedule (announcements are made of any changes ahead of time)
- a *thorough* introduction of new activities and materials available
- an organized and age-appropriate environment that offers interesting and varied materials for children to use and explore and makes them easily accessible.

With these guidelines in mind, here is the way a teacher at the Greenfield Center School organized the planning process for the children in his class.

The six year olds in the primary classroom, already familiar with their room, the areas, the activities and the materials available, arrive each morning to find the "have-to" blackboard full of names and activities. They each eagerly look for their name under such headings as Group Work, Art, Independent Math, Discovery, and note to themselves and their friends their have-to's for the morning. Next stop is usually the morning's *News and Announcement*

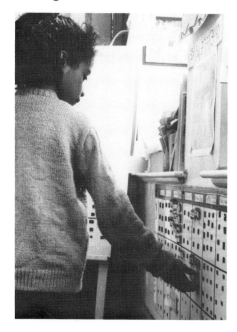

chart where they carefully read the simple sentences to see if there might possibly be any new or special activities occurring that day. By now, the room is humming with children's voices as they talk over ideas with friends and their teacher about possible "choice" activities that will fill up their morning. Some children come to school with definite plans already made about activities and friends to work with, perhaps the plan being made the day before, or on the way to school. Others need the stimulation of being at school and sharing ideas with friends before they can begin to think about their morning activities. And there are still others, who need the guidance of teacher suggestions or questioning to help them sort out their options and make a choice.

THE PLAN BOOK

The children each take out their plan book, which is a collection of five plan sheets stapled together with a cover, made at the start of each week, and find a place where they can comfortably sit to write their plans. However, children do not write out their full plan until after meeting when they've had an opportunity to hear all the *News and Announcements* for the day and their teacher has reviewed the list of various "have-to's." If there is a new math manipulative available or a new rock to study at the discovery table, this is the time when their teacher introduces it and talks of its care and possibilities for use. After meeting children put their names on a choice board under the name of an area in the room where they plan to work first. In this way children can adjust the order of their activities planned to meet the space limits of each area. For example, if only four can work in the drama area, and four names have already been posted, Kim and Jeff who would like to work there as their first choice must now rearrange their plans because the area is full. They can plan to use the drama area second in their morning. The large work time of the morning is generally divided into 3 time periods of about ½ hour each. This allows for children to take turns in some of the most popular areas that operate best because the number of children playing at any one time is limited. However, some of the areas in the room can absorb infinite numbers of children and therefore are *not* regulated by time periods. It is extremely important for children to have the time to work at their own pace.

Now that they have chosen their first activity for the day, the children go back to their plan books and write

out their plans taking into consideration their have-to's and their choices. The teacher has already spent a few moments before meeting with each child discussing plans, making needed suggestions and asking questions. The final step in the process is for each child to share his or her written plan with the teacher. He carefully reads each plan and when it is completed responds with a positive word about it. The children quickly put their plan books away and with intent and purpose head towards their first activity.

There are, in fact, three parts to the planning process. We have looked at the first which is the actual planning itself. Next comes the "working" part in which children carry out their plans. Not every plan or project is expected to work. Figuring out why it doesn't work may, when it is deliberately examined, yield the most important insights and understanding. It is the task of the teacher to guide children not just toward activity as an end in itself, but toward intelligent activity. In working with the ages five to seven, there are characteristics of each age that teachers need to keep in mind in helping them to take risks and stretch towards that intelligent activity.

CARRYING OUT THEIR PLANS
Five Year Olds

- can easily be distracted from or simply forget plan: need reminders of plan or guidance in rewriting or rearranging plan
- can completely change plan in midstream without discussing change with other children involved: need guidance in learning how to cooperate with others in planning

Six Year Olds

- can now handle short and simple independent assignments in reading and math, but will sometimes get distracted before completion: need to have a quiet nondistracting place in room to work on these assignments
- can be very speedy: desire to do is greater than ability to finish
- can often start an activity but will leave half-way through and go on to other acitvity: need guidance in choosing activities that can be completed within reasonable time and in remaining with activity until it is completed; and/or need guidance in planning how to remember and complete all activity over a period of time, working in short intervals and planning for storage.

Seven Year Olds

- can get very involved in one activity and lose sight of the rest of the plan,

not having time to complete: need guidance in pacing themselves so they can complete daily plan
- love longer-term projects; however can get so involved that they get stuck and cannot move on to completion of project: need guidance in planning appropriate amount of time to work on and complete project and in setting some goals for what *is* completion of the project.

RESULTS

The third and final step in the planning process is "Results" in which there is time for summary and evaluation. Each day children are given time to review their plan and their activities of the day, share learning and accomplishments with peer and teacher, think about next steps for on-going projects, and in general, reflect on their feelings during the day. Children are asked to take responsibility for their learning and their activities through self-evaluation and examination of work done. There is also time to share projects worked on with peers and to listen to their suggestions and ideas. Children learn to help each other examine work, taking risks and feeling support and pride. Evaluation is done in a way that is appropriate to each age level. Fives color in, on their plan sheet, all the activities accomplished and verbally share with peers and/or teacher events of the day that made them feel good, excited, mad, scared, unhappy, frustrated, etc. Sixes color in all their activities accomplished and begin to write a sentence that explains how they felt about their day. Sevens write very briefly about their accomplishments of the day and a sentence or two sharing their feelings of the day.

The teacher responds immediately to the five year old's "Results," verbally supporting and guiding the child's thinking about the day and possible applications to future plans. With the six and seven year old, the teacher can respond in writing directly on the plansheet. This dialogue between teacher and child fosters the active, respectful "give and take" necessary in a developmental curriculum.

Scheduling in the Developmental Classroom

In a developmental curriculum the daily schedule requires as much attention from the teacher as does the organization of the planning process for the children and the structuring of the areas and materials in the environment. The daily schedule provides a consistency and an external structure that helps children to develop their own inner control and an ability to plan. The daily schedule makes the children's day organized, predictable and therefore, safe. Children and teacher both can actively plan their work, and carry it out in an organized environment with sufficient time. The daily schedule also allows for a variety and balance of activities to occur.

Each age level demands a different kind of schedule which meets the need of that age. The daily schedule also allows for a variety and balance of activities and groupings (whole group/small group/individual).

Five Year Olds Need	Six Year Olds Need	Seven Year Olds Need
• short whole group meetings (15-20 min.), can go longer if meeting is active	• longer meetings (20-30 min.), must have active parts	• longer meetings (30 min.), whole group lessons are easier
• alternate quiet and active activities; small groups work best for instruction	• alternate quiet and active activities, some whole group, more small group	• longer work periods, some quiet, balance of whole group/small group/individual work
• long time period to plan	• to plan quietly under supervision	• to plan more quickly and independently than sixes
• to evaluate half day only at beginning	• to evaluate whole day	• to evaluate whole day
• long time periods for transitions— clean-up, arrival, getting ready to go out or for lunch	• some transitions with longer time (clean-up) but in general move more quickly	• shorter transition times with lots of warning
• organized physical activity, free play outdoors each day	• organized physical activity in afternoon	• organized physical activity at least twice a day
• relaxing activity to end the day, part can be whole group	• relaxing activity to end the day, part can be whole group	• relaxing activity to end the day, whole group works well

Every teacher must then decide what schedule best fits her students within the external structure of her school. When giving children the freedom to be active, responsible planners and learners, a teacher needs to anticipate changes in schedule, giving enough notice to her students so that they, too, can be prepared.

We have included 2 sample schedules from our school as a guide to teachers thinking of using a developmental approach to their teaching. They serve to demonstrate how various schedules can be organized to meet the needs of children ages 5 to 7.

Sample Schedule for Fives and Sixes

8:30	Arrival, Greetings, Begin Planning
8:45	Morning Meeting: Daily Chart Activities, Math Ritual, Singing, Sharing (shorter time at beginning of year)
9:15	Complete Plan in Planbook
9:30	Work Period: Choices, Have-to's, Small Groups in Math, Reading Conferences
10:30	Clean up
10:45	Meeting: Language Arts Focus
11:00	Whole Class Writing Time (mid-year)
11:30	Outdoor Games
12:00	Lunch
12:30	Story/Shared Reading/Singing
12:45	Reading: Partner, Individual, Conferences, Small Group
1:15	Work Period: Social Studies/Science Work, Choices, Have-to's, Math Groups
2:00	Clean up
2:15	Outdoor Free Play
2:30	Results, Quiet Time/Representing Meeting
3:00	Dismissal

Sample Schedule for Sevens

8:30	Arrival, Greetings, Planning
9:00	Morning Meeting: Daily Chart Activities, Math Ritual, Singing Sharing
9:30	Theme Work Period (Social Studies/Science Focus): Choices, Have-to's (Whole Group/Small Group/Individual)
10:00	Outside Physical Activity
10:15	Math Work Period: Choices, Have-to's (Whole Group/Small Group, Individual)
10:45	Whole Class Writing
11:15	Clean up
11:30	Outdoor Games
12:00	Lunch
12:30	Story/Shared Reading/Singing
12:45	Reading: Conferences, Small Groups, Partner, Individual
1:30	Work Period: Choices, Have-to's
2:15	Clean up
2:30	Results, Quiet Time/Representing Meeting
3:00	Dismissal

Sample Plans

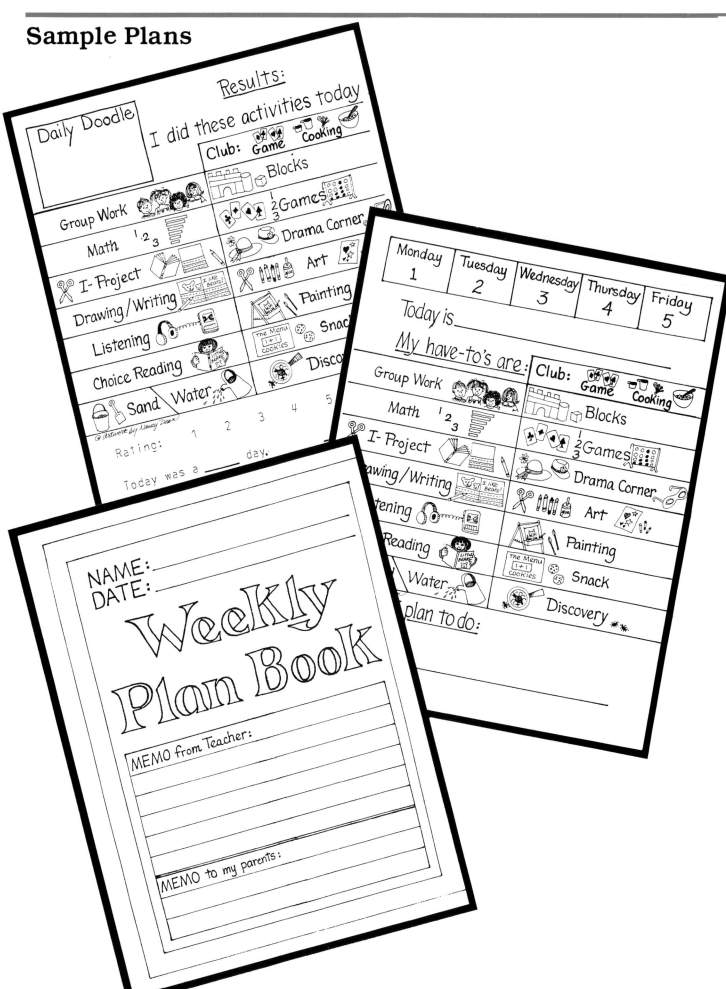

Daily Doodle

Results:
I did these activities today

Club: Game Cooking

Group Work
Blocks
Math 1 2 3
1 2 3 Games
I- Project
Drama Corner
Drawing/Writing
Art
Listening
Painting
Choice Reading
The Menu 1+1 cookies Snack
Sand Water
Discovery

© Artwork by Nancy Dean

Rating: 1 2 3 4 5

Today was a _____ day.

Monday 1	Tuesday 2	Wednesday 3	Thursday 4	Friday 5

Today is _____

My have-to's are: Club: Game Cooking

Group Work
Blocks
Math 1 2 3
1 2 3 Games
I- Project
Drama Corner
Drawing/Writing
Art
Listening
Painting
Reading
The Menu 1+1 cookies Snack
Water
Discovery

I plan to do:

_____

NAME: _____
DATE: _____

Weekly Plan Book

MEMO from Teacher:

MEMO to my parents:

Results: What happened today?

A book I'm reading _____

Rating: 1 2 3 4 5 6 7 8 9 10

Results: _____

Teacher's Comment

name: _____
date: _____

Weekly Plan Book

memo to Ellen: _____

memo from Ellen: _____

Monday 1	Tuesday 2	Wednesday 3	Thursday 4	Friday 5

Today is _____
My plan:

1) _____

2) _____

3) _____

4) _____

Quiet Time 5) _____ © Artwork by Nancy Dean

Independent Reading	Independent Math
Theme Work	Blocks
Drama	Arts
Writing	Games
Listening	Tutoring
Group Work	Science

MAKING CHANGES

- **FIRST STEP:**
  A Visit to a Classroom
- **WHERE TO GO FROM HERE:**
  Flow Chart
- **APPROACHES THAT WORK:**
  I Am Needed—The Child as Tutor
  The Developmental Curriculum Goes Home
  What Did You Do in School Today?
- **A REFLECTION:**
  When a Teacher Looks Inside
- **RESOURCES:**
  Bibliography
  People Who Can Help
- **POSTSCRIPT:**
  "The Sand-Collar Curriculum"

The First Step:
A Visit to a Classroom

Jonathan, arriving early to school, strides into the classroom, a serious, intense set to his stance. He scans the room, gestures hello to his teacher and strides over to a sprawling block structure. His jacket and lunch pail slip to the floor as he bends over the building. "Yes, the door must be bigger," he remarks, carefully lifting off a platform to expose the outer perimeters. Each attempt to enlarge the opening threatens the fit of the corners, causing apparent frustration as he assembles and arranges this side—then that. Finally, releasing a great sigh, springing to his feet so that he just escapes tumbling into lunch pail and jacket, he scurries off to the block shelves.

"See, Ricky," he calls to a child playing inobtrusively with a neighboring building. "This is what I need."

Ricky returns a calm appraisal.

Jonathan stacks the smaller-size blocks in a column, furtively adding from an adjacent building to complete his own wall. He replaces the platform ceiling, the task finished. A pleased smile alights his face. From his jacket pocket he produces a red fire engine truck which he positions in front of the recently repaired fire station doors. Providing a proper siren whir, he easily drives the truck into its garage, fitting neatly through its entrance way.

"If you getta fire, I'll be there in exo time," he announces in full voice. Jonathan's day is well underway.

Others are arriving singly and in small groups. Coats are quickly hung in the outer hall, lunch boxes nestled into a shelf and plan books removed from a bin. Lisa comes in skipping, leading her father who appears behind a large cardboard box. In no time, a curious crowd peers into the mysterious box. A garter snake, found slithering about the family backyard, was too fascinating just to leave at home. "Please can I take it to school?"

The teacher immediately sets Lisa to cleaning out a tank. "It will crawl out of that box," Jack says knowingly. "We need something with a top."

"But then it won't be able to breathe," adds Cindy.

A flow of questions and information accompany the watchful gathering. "Snakes eat frogs," says Tony.

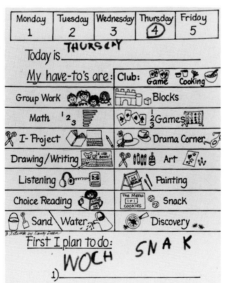

"No, they don't. They eat potato chips," asserts the giggling Jackie.

"Ms. Clayton can we go find some frogs for the snake to eat?"

Preparations for the temporary home rivet the in-comers' interest. Lisa writes, "LISA'S GRTR SNAK" and pastes it on the tank. Ms. Clayton disappears from the room, momentarily returning with several books about snakes. She props one book on a stand by the snake's tank.

Routines continue. And children go to their planning.

Myra scrutinizes the blackboard. "Oh, Noooo... I have I-Math today." (Independent Math Sheets)

"I love my Facts book" (a workbook), "don't you," says Cindy.

"Wanna plan with me?" Jessie asks Myra. "Let's do drama first." Visits to the snake, the blackboard and casual greetings occur side by side. Jonathan still absorbed in his fire station needs several promptings to put away his coat and attend to morning jobs. Jeremy, too, is whisked away from the snake, but then returns with his plan book, which he holds on his lap as he alternates writing and looking. Plan 1, on Jeremy's plan sheet says, "Wach Snak."

Melissa is busy recounting last night's adventures, her plan book ignored in front of her. Ms. Clayton circulates, checking plans and greeting her children. "I see you are going on with your illustrations today. I can't wait to see them," she tells Joey. "I think it would be a good idea to start with I-Math, Maggie. Remember you didn't want to let it wait till afternoon."

"Did you get your new puppy? Would you like to share this morning?" she asks Anya.

"Do you think I could make some food for my supermarket?" asks Timmy. They have a brief conference about Timmy's project. Ms. Clayton needs to remind Tony to reread the blackboard. He will need to switch LEGO® blocks and group work, she counsels. Someone else reminds the teacher that *she* forgot to include his name for Reading Group. Chris tries to figure out when Adam can play "Trouble" with him, and Molly remembers she has tutoring today.

The children are adept at scheduling their "Have-to's," listed *each morning on the blackboard, their choices, integrating daily, predictable tasks, ongoing and special activities. By 9:00* all the plans are done. The group heads off for morning meeting.

Melissa's Plan:
(1) Drama with Jessie
(2) Reading Group
(3) I-Math

Jackie's Plan:
(1) Draw the Snake
(2) I-Math
(3) Listen to tape and play LEGO® blocks

Morning Meeting

The group gathers in a circle on the floor, each resting on his own small rug-cushion marking out a place. The meeting begins with a song. Today they sing a favorite about the well-loved convention of eating "peanut-butter with jam," and then peanut-butter and the wildest, gooeyest, most fantastic and unreasonable combinations ever the mind can fathom. The group conspires to shock and reach new ridiculous heights. Today, of course, the snake appears in verse after verse. The "horrid" additions are copied into a chart-size song book and resung together. Humor, music and invention affirm the group, initiating the first gathering of the day to set a tone. Meetings are highly deliberate, purposeful vehicles to convey both academic and social goals.

After the song, information about the day is reviewed. Someone tells the date: "Today is Thursday, April 14." The sentence, spoken in full, is written in full on the chart. "I'm feeling a bit sleepy this morning. Can someone remind me what sound Thursday begins with and what two letters make that sound?" Ms. Clayton asks. Hands go up. The teacher writes THURS_____, leaving the work unfinished. A chorus of thrilled gasps.

"Ms. Clayton, you forgot..."

"Oh, yes," she agrees and inserts the letters Danny uttered. Her queries tap the most well-established, repetitive skills, as well as draw attention to new items to learn. A range is so carefully geared to include a wide spread of abilities and levels.

Molly reads the calendar date.

"What can you tell me about the number 14?" Ms. Clayton asks.

Myra knows that 14 is 7 and 7. Andy knows that 2 of the 7's are 14. Jonathan says that 13 and 1 are 14. Danny thinks there are 14 chairs in the room. Jessie reports that her babysitter is 14. On the 14th of April, the children know that Maggie is first all day; they know that Aaron brought a snack; they know that there is an All-School meeting in the afternoon;

News and Announcements
Maggie is first.
Today is Thurs____.
April 14th, 1984.
Aaron brought snack.
We have All-School Meeting.
7 + 7 = 14
13 + 1 = 14

How do snakes move?
Predictions

they know that team 3 plays team 4 at recess; they know that Lisa brought a real snake to school. An animated conversation about snakes begins. Joey tells about poisonous rattlers. Melissa saw a snake in her yard, too. Adam's father has a snake skin. Jackie saw a movie with a fiendish boa constrictor. Billy begins to curl his lip to reveal fangs and makes a sly hissing sound. Erect children curl over into S crouching, ready to slither. Their bodies and faces coil into "snake-ness." After a few moments, Ms. Clayton asks a question, redirecting the focus to real rather than improvised knowledge. Her question provokes observations; "I wonder if snakes have feet or just how they move. Jackie was worried that our snake might crawl out of his box if we didn't attach a lid. How would it do that?" Andy thinks the notion of a snake with feet is silly. But then adds, "Maybe they have hundreds of tiny feet like a centipede. I caught a centipede once." Ricky imitates a moving snake, squirming across the circle. Myra offers another pantomine, arching then contracting in rhythmic precision. Ms. Clayton writes the question on the chart: HOW DO SNAKES MOVE? They decide to investigate the way a snake moves by observing closely. A list of "Predictions" is written on the left-hand side of the chart, leaving the right side for reporting on the results of the study. Other questions are considered such as "Can a snake really move up the side of a wall?" "How fast?" "Can it move backwards?" The teacher also lists guidelines for observing and ways to record. (Some children will draw what they see. Others may locate or check key vocabulary. Others will write phrases and sentences. Some will dictate to a partner a special discovery. Her expectations are not uniform.) Rules for handling and care of the animal are stated firmly.

Anya taps Ms. Clayton's arm, a worried look on her face. "You forgot about me," she whispered. "Yes, I did," Ms. Clayton acknowledges. "There's still time. Would you like to tell us now?" Relieved, Anya stands up and informs the group that she just got a puppy. "Questions and comments?" Anya asks. A flurry of questions. Anya answers carefully. Anya's news is added to the chart. Children take turns reading and then play a short word game. "I'm thinking of a word beginning with 's' sound that means how a snake moves." Anya jumps up to find the word, reads it and now it's her turn to ask a riddle.

The meeting comes to an end with each child telling what he will do for his first work period. Quietly the children disperse, tucking away mats and setting off to different areas, different tasks and activities.

Working

The transition from meeting as a whole class, to working in pairs, alone, or small groups is gradual. A slow change of pace is preferred. Gentle chatter, a low hum of business and motion accompanies the steady, sure drift into the work periods. The flow represents the strong co-ordination between the intuitions and wishes of the child, the planned and organized environment, the structure and attention of the teacher. Routine and spontaneity exist side by side. By mid-year, visitors marvel at the independence and self-direction of the students.

Several children are already setting up shop in the drama area. Articles from the costume trunk are going on display, jewelry for "fancy parties" is to be the special attraction of one department and Melissa's sign indicates there is a "Shu sale." "Dress stores do so sell shoes," insists Melissa.

Jessie wants to make a big sign for the shop. There is a pause in the preparations as the three girls defend their choices of names.

Other children scurry over to the block area, some to continue work on their buildings, some to construct anew. A defined limit, with a set rotation, insures a comfortable number in this very favorite area.

Ms. Clayton is helping to set up the discovery table for observations, supplying a few magnifying glasses, measuring tools, a poster with printed questions and vocabulary terms they might need to use, a book propped open to text and picture, a spacious area to watch and draw. Meanwhile, her reading group has formed, at a nearby round table, books and folders in hand, retrieved from the "shoe-bag" cubby.

Josh brings over a bucket of colored rods (CUISENAIRE® rods), where he joins a group doing *I-Math*. "Here's your folder," calls Adam, gathering utensils for his buddies.

Aaron takes a piece of drawing paper, a large black marker and prints out instruction for snack:

POPCORN 3 + 3 – 4 CUPS

He grins, apparently satisfied with such an equation, and tapes the message to the wooden snack sign which he places neatly before the big bag of popcorn.

Chris selects a book, sprawls out on the meeting rug, begins to read.

Timmy finds the can of PLASTICINE® modeling material and carefully lays out newspaper before beginning to roll out balls of colored clay.

"Want some help?" Anya asks as she studies the colored balls. She continues to wander, passing the drama

area and fingering a pair of soft white gloves.

"You can't take that. We're using it," snaps Molly. "This is a dress store."

Anya purses her lips, frowns and says, "OK. OK. I just wanted to buy these. How much?"

Molly, satisfied, replies, "$50."

Myra overhearing, pipes in, "$50? They're 50 cents."

Snatching up a pocketbook, Anya announces that she is going to make some money for the store. The others nod in agreement. Skipping off, she spies her name on the Choice Board for games. Aloud, but to herself, "I guess I better change my plan."

Jeremy gathers his reading folder and goes to sit next to Joey, who is laying out the special set of colored pens used only for illustrating published books. "It's awful gross, I know," he grins sheepishly, partially concealing and partially showing off his meticulous drawing of a fiery dragon. Jeremy does battle with the fictional monster and the two friends enact a pencil duel. "I'm gonna do a pirate now. I'm sooo bad at pirates."

"Pirates were real, you know," adds Jeremy with authority. "I read about Captain Kidd. He hid treasures and made people walk a plank and swim to Florida."

Jeremy opens his red folder, thumbs through several worksheets tucked into a pocket; he finds one with a big colored smile and written comment which says, "Good Job, Jeremy. I like your story about the fight."—a mark and comment from his teacher. He looks at it for a while. From the other pocket, he draws out a new sheet. "Oh, God," he mumbles, shaking his head, as if in disbelief. "I have to do so much work."

Chris and Aaron squat in the block area, facing each other, as they begin a bumper car race, increasing in pitch as sound effects are added to the ram/drive action. A car speeds into Billy's building. Billy grabs it, clenching it in a tight fist high above Aaron's head. Aaron lurches and scuffles. Ms. Clayton, with stern, quiet voice, directs Chris and Aaron to a five-minute time-out suggesting they decide on a plan before returning to the blocks.

Billy, holding on to the car, runs it across the surface of his bridge, watching it fall—Kaplunk—to the floor as it reaches the end of the roadway. He is proud of the bridge's height and pointed arches which span the lofty columns.

Billy had taken a holiday trip to New Jersey, crossing the George Washington Bridge and this was the "Gorg Washingtn Brge" as his bright lettered sign proclaimed. "It has 2 levels," he boasted, "I went on the top." For days he had worked on his construction, suffering the repeated frustrations as footsteps sent vibrations across the floor, dislodging or toppling a section. Each new fix-up had added to the solidness of the structure, but still cars "flew up" and "flew down." Billy fit a ramp securely to a flat and leaned the blocks against the roadway. Shaking his head, he dropped them back to floor level and joined up more roadway. Turning to Aaron, who had recently returned, Billy said, "You pay a dollar to go on the bridge." He hands Aaron the car. "Pay me a dollar and you can go to New Jersey." Aaron grins, calls out, "Wait a sec." Moments later he is back waving a dollar fresh off Anya's money press. The traffic awaits the completion of a tollbooth.

Later, Ms. Clayton will ask Billy to "share his bridge." There will be a "brainstorming" session to explore ways to solve the problem of elevation. Pictures and perhaps a field trip may offer or extend their factual base. The group expresses conflicting urges—to adapt magical solutions, with flying cars, turbo-propelled space-age fantasies and a growing interest in mechanical causations of the physical world. They will read *The Big Gray Bridge* at story time and compare the beautiful water color illustrations in the story with Billy's model. Billy embraces the book, reading it over and over to himself during quiet time, tracing his memories and relishing his experience.

Adam is making "trains" with rods. He has a teacher-made booklet, with printed equations.

$$\boxed{} + W = P$$

"What makes purple?" he mutters, translating the funny hieroglyphics from the page before him. He dips into the bin containing lots of the colored rod-like blocks and picks out a light green which he deftly lines up with the white, measuring them against the purple. He smiles and exclaims aloud, "Soo easy." Later in the term, or perhaps next year, Adam will be taught that the rods have a number equivalency. Now, he explores the operations and properties unrestricted by a numerical value. He writes the results in his book.

$$\boxed{Lg} + W = P$$

He glances over to check Emily's work. Reading her problems, he says, "I got that one. It's exo!" Emily nods, in obvious agreement, but without interrupting her work. Across, Jackie

has begun a long trail of orange rods spanning the horizontal surface of his table. He grabs up more orange rods. "Can I have your orange?" he asks Emily. Emily eyes the orange line and adds an orange herself. "You're going to fall off the end of the world," she warns happily, as he reaches the end of the table.

"I'm going to make a train all the way over to the sink."

"Wanna help?"

The three busily link rods, end to end, crawling across the floor.

"Oh, no! We're in trouble! NO MORE ORANGES!" wails Emily.

"Let's ask Ms. Clayton if we can borrow some," suggests Jackie.

Adam is quietly substituting a red and brown, comparing their sum to the orange and seeing that they are equal. He says with confidence, "Yes, they're the same." He speeds on with the job of "Sink Ho!" The others quickly pick up the idea, form trains of different colors, always in proportion to the orange (thus discovering subsets of 10).

"We have hundreds and hundreds," they cry.

"I wonder if we could make a train all the way around the school?"

"That would be billions and billions."

"Infinity," says Jackie.

A foursome comprises the first reading group of the morning. Waiting for Ms. Clayton, they examine their latest book, "The Storm," fifth in the Griffen Pirate series. "I hate lightning. Don't you?" one asks. The teacher sits down and joins the discussion underway on storms. She helps to focus on specific details, which she knows will key into the text. New vocabulary words are discussed and written on file cards. Each child takes a turn reading aloud. There is a groan when the lightning hits the ship, a giggle when the clumsy, clownish Roderick falls overboard, a gasp when the next ship nears the treacherous rocks. "Watch out Blue Pirate," says the wise Matthew. Together they complete about half the 20-page book, reading comfortably at a primer level. Sight words are reviewed and added to word-rings. There is a short instructional sequence on the 'ight' pattern. To conclude they return to the subject of storms, recalling and hearing personal episodes. Ms. Clayton assigns them a task to complete on their own. She tells them to look at the sky and decide if it might storm. They are to draw the sky and write a weather report. She leaves them to go on with their work. In their red "I-Reading" folders, she inserts a worksheet for the next day, reviewing new words, practicing patterns and writing answers to questions of content. "I hope it storms," Tracy says to Matthew, "I see a cloud. Do you?"

Ricky strolls over to the snack table, studies the message. Trotting over to the water table he picks up a large measuring cup and takes it over to Aaron after dropping in some popcorn. "It says a cup." he tells Aaron with a smirk. Including his friend in his joke, he says, "Let's get a cup of popcorn."

Lisa sits quite still allowing the snake to coil and uncoil about her wrist. "I think it likes me." Gently stroking its underbelly, "Maybe it has tiny feet inside."

A soft bell rings, alerting the children that the first working period is now over. The morning work time is divided into three periods, although these periods are *not* rigidly implemented or enforced. Some children will now put away blocks so that others may use them. Melissa knows that she has to retire from her dress shop to attend her group, perhaps to resume later or perhaps to follow her original plan. Other children will play a board game, cards, listen to tapes, work on their Independent Math tasks, etc. The plan is a structure—it is not a blueprint. Children are learning to take responsibility, but it is understood that they will proceed in this manner as well as at their own pace. Shifts are evident even in day-to-day management. Ms. Clayton will calmly remind some that they need to do their "have-to's." She will leave others to face the consequence of an Incompletion—perhaps to postpone an afternoon choice. Some will need to be sent back to an earlier station to tidy up or do a better job of putting away that game. Some, particularly the sixes will simply forget their plan, and ignore their tag on the choice board, given the still undifferentiated nature of time concepts. Another child, all intense effort and rapt attention as she mixes the blues and purples of a night time sky, is permitted to continue her painting. Starts and stops are not always to be regulated by external demands. Choices, too, may shift mid-stream, mid-morning. The spontaneous initiatives of the young child are balanced with externally channeled industry and action.

A few may flit. A watchful concern is paid to the "flitters." Behavior is viewed, however, in terms of individual history and patterns. One child may need additional teacher supervision and direction. Yet another may need more time to test and try out the environment, while adult intervention is ready—if necessary—to prevent destructive diversions. Observation informs the teacher as to the consistency and persistence of diffi-

cult or troublesome behavior.

The Morning Plan is, in fact, a magnificent duet between teachers and children. The voices, not equally loud or sure, sing in tune. Choices are balanced with "Have-to's." Independent work with group work. Quiet activity intersperses with active, noisy activity. The firm grasp of the pencil relaxes with the loose roll of the dice. The teacher sees to the environment, its possibilities and opportunities, its schedule and equipment. Her arrangements are in concert with the knowledge and expectations of her children, giving support to the child's most natural, wholesome and spirited drive to learn.

Examining the Record

The visitor is asked to reread the Narrative and to reorganize it and cluster it according to the questions outlined below. Colored markers or crayons may be used to underline for the more visual or concrete learners.

■ Use the Narrative to locate five examples of specific classroom management by the teacher (underline in orange).

■ Use the Narrative to locate five different materials and/or manipulatives children use during the morning (underline in red).

■ Use the Narrative to locate five examples of reading instruction (underline in purple).

■ Use the Narrative to locate five examples of children planning and managing portions of their morning (underline in blue).

Sample Reports

SOCIAL STUDIES/SCIENCE

Group Focus—Science:

The children are learning ways to work and think like scientists. For observations they work in small groups to discuss what they notice about the object they are studying and discuss what questions they have. Then they will draw what they see and write about it. The goals are to observe more intently, making full use of their senses and to explore the objects and/or the environment.

Group Focus—Social Studies:

The goals are to investigate real-life topics or "themes" as a class. This will include taking field trips, class readings, discussions, writing and visitors. Their new knowledge is expressed through their block buildings, art work and dramatic play.

Individual Progress:

	Mid Year	Year's End		Mid Year	Year's End
1. Explores interest and shows knowledge by: observing questioning experimenting using detail	___	___	2. Retains information from: listening activities and projects discussion	___	___
			3. Will follow guided inquiry to solve problems and extend understanding	___	___

COMMENTS:

MATHEMATICS

Group Focus:

Children use arithmetic in their daily lives. Our special focus has been based on the use of concrete materials such as unifix cubes, junk boxes, attribute blocks, and unit blocks to firmly establish an ever increasing understanding of number, pattern and relationships. Children have also practiced writing and reading numbers, and making sets. As a class, the children are introduced to and expected to explore the mathematical concepts involved in block building, graphing, measuring, time and money.

Individual Progress:

SKILLS (5's)

	Mid Year	Year's End
1. Vocabulary of size and position	___	___
2. Sorting and matching #'s to sets	___	___
3. Counting 1 to 20	___	___
4. Recognizing shapes and spacial relationships	___	___
5. Recognizing numerals 0 - 10 and writing them	___	___
6. Classifications according to color, shape, size by 1 attribute	___	___
7. Identifying and reproducing simple patterns	___	___

COMMENTS:

SKILLS (5-6's)

	Mid Year	Year's End
1. Comparing and sequencing	___	___
2. Grouping and regrouping sets up to 10	___	___
3. Graphing	___	___
4. Writing numbers up to 20	___	___
5. Counting by tens	___	___
6. Beginning experience with all operations using rods	___	___
7. Addition and subtraction from #'s up to 10 using manipulatives	___	___
8. Story problems with + and -	___	___
9. Classification with 1 and 2 attributes	___	___
10. Identifying, reproducing, creating complex patterns	___	___

SKILLS (6-7's)

	Mid Year	Year's End
1. Counting up to 100, by fives, by tens	___	___
2. Recognizing numbers up to 100 and writing them	___	___
3. Place value for 1's and 10's	___	___
4. 1 and 2 digit addition and subtraction	___	___
5. Equations with simple multiplication, addition, subtraction using rods	___	___
6. Grouping & regrouping up to 20	___	___
7. Money, recognizing coins; making change for a dollar	___	___
8. Classification with 2-3 attributes	___	___

EVALUATION REPORT

GREENFIELD CENTER SCHOOL
71 MONTAGUE CITY ROAD
GREENFIELD, MA 01301

NAME	CLASS	PERIOD

Key M = MASTERY: Does carefully and thoughtfully on a regular basis
P = PROGRESS: Shows steady improvement and growth
H = HELP: Needs frequent direction from teacher
N = Skill or behavior NOT displayed

PLANNING, WORKING, REPRESENTING

Group Focus:

At this level all children are learning to recognize and record their daily have-to's and choices in our room are Group Work and plan for their first activity. The have-to's and choices in our room are Group Work (math, drawing and writing or reading) assigned Independent Work (in math, drawing and writing or reading), free play at the Math Bug, Sand/Water, Drama Corner, Blocks, or Art, instructional Art, Block Project, Choice Reading or Games in the loft, Tutoring and Snack. As the children move into recording their Independent Work they will be responsible for returning it to the teacher via the Finished Work Box. They are expected to clean up after themselves in each activity and in the two major class clean-ups. "Results" give them an opportunity to think back over their day, record all their activities they did and begin to learn how to evaluate what makes a good day or a bad day. Most days also include at least one "sharing time" when they are able to represent some of their school work. The children are also learning new strategies in working together in small and large groups.

Individual Progress:

	Mid-Year	Year's End
PLANNING		
1. Follows planning routine	___	___
2. Makes plans in cooperation with other children	___	___
3. Plans activities that last more than one work period	___	___
WORKING		
1. Knows and participates in room routines: meetings games quiet time clean up	___	___
2. Follows daily plan	___	___
3. Makes appropriate choices in room	___	___
4. Initiates a variety of projects	___	___
5. Works with persistance	___	___
6. Works independently	___	___
7. Works cooperatively in peer groups	___	___
8. Works cooperatively in teacher-led groups	___	___

COMMENTS:

REPRESENTING (the sharing of experiences, work, learning and ideas)

	Mid Year	Year's End
1. Will represent to teachers	___	___
2. Will represent to peers	___	___
3. Will represent to whole class	___	___
4. Represents through:	Mid-Year	Year's End

EVALUATION

1. Evaluates work for completion
2. Evaluates day's work and experiences and substantiates it

EVALUATION of student progress in a developmental program requires careful attention to all aspects of growth and development.

Our "report cards" combine a checklist and narrative approach matched to developmental expectations in each area.

All report forms, including our own, should improve and change over time to better match the curriculum and reflect age-appropriate activity. We are indebted to the High Scope Foundation, Ypsilanti, Michigan, whose own reporting forms have served as the model for our evaluations.

Developmental Sixes and Sevens

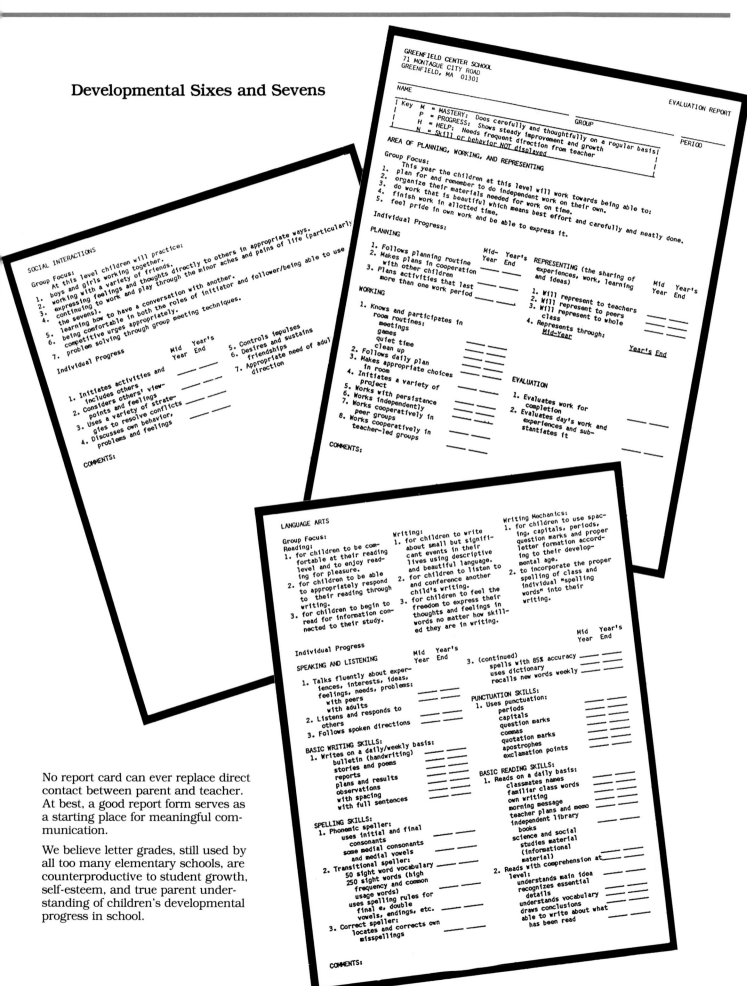

GREENFIELD CENTER SCHOOL
71 MONTAGUE CITY ROAD
GREENFIELD, MA 01301

NAME _____

EVALUATION REPORT

Key M = MASTERY: Does carefully and thoughtfully on a regular basis
     P = PROGRESS: Shows steady improvement and growth
     H = HELP: Needs frequent direction from teacher
     N = Skill or behavior NOT displayed

GROUP _____

PERIOD _____

AREA OF PLANNING, WORKING, AND REPRESENTING

Group Focus:
This year the children at this level will work towards being able to:
1. plan for and remember to do independent work on their own.
2. organize their materials needed for work on time.
3. do work that is beautiful which means best effort and carefully and neatly done.
4. finish work in allotted time.
5. feel pride in own work and be able to express it.

Individual Progress:

PLANNING
1. Follows planning routine
2. Makes plans in cooperation with other children
3. Plans activities that last more than one work period

WORKING
1. Knows and participates in room routines:
   meetings
   games
   quiet time
   clean up
2. Follows daily plan
3. Makes appropriate choices in room
4. Initiates a variety of project
5. Works with persistance
6. Works independently
7. Works cooperatively in peer groups
8. Works cooperatively in teacher-led groups

COMMENTS:

REPRESENTING (the sharing of experiences, work, learning and ideas)
1. Will represent to teachers
2. Will represent to peers
3. Will represent to whole class
4. Represents through:
   Mid-Year

EVALUATION
1. Evaluates work for completion
2. Evaluates day's work and experiences and substantiates it

SOCIAL INTERACTIONS

Group Focus:
At this level children will practice:
1. boys and girls working together.
2. working with a variety of friends.
3. expressing feelings and thoughts directly to others in appropriate ways.
4. continuing to work and play through the minor aches and pains of life (particularly the sevens).
5. learning how to have a conversation with another.
6. being comfortable in both the roles of initiator and follower/being able to use competitive urges appropriately.
7. problem solving through group meeting techniques.

Individual Progress

1. Initiates activities and includes others
2. Considers others' viewpoints and feelings
3. Uses a variety of strategies to resolve conflicts
4. Discusses own behavior, problems and feelings

5. Controls impulses
6. Desires and sustains friendships
7. Appropriate need of adult direction

COMMENTS:

LANGUAGE ARTS

Group Focus:
Reading:
1. for children to be comfortable at their reading level and to enjoy reading for pleasure.
2. for children to be able to appropriately respond to their reading through writing.
3. for children to begin to read for information connected to their study.

Writing:
1. for children to write about small but significant events in their lives using descriptive and beautiful language.
2. for children to listen to and conference another child's writing.
3. for children to feel the freedom to express their thoughts and feelings in words no matter how skilled they are in writing.

Writing Mechanics:
1. for children to use spacing, capitals, periods, question marks and proper letter formation according to their developmental age.
2. to incorporate the proper spelling of class and individual "spelling words" into their writing.

Individual Progress

SPEAKING AND LISTENING
1. Talks fluently about experiences, interests, ideas, feelings, needs, problems:
   with peers
   with adults
2. Listens and responds to others
3. Follows spoken directions

BASIC WRITING SKILLS:
1. Writes on a daily/weekly basis:
   bulletin (handwriting)
   stories and poems
   reports
   plans and results
   observations
   with spacing
   with full sentences

SPELLING SKILLS:
1. Phonemic speller:
   uses initial and final consonants
   some medial consonants and medial vowels
2. Transitional speller:
   50 sight word vocabulary
   250 sight words (high frequency and common usage words)
   uses spelling rules for final e, double vowels, endings, etc.
3. Correct speller:
   locates and corrects own misspellings

3. (continued)
   spells with 85% accuracy
   uses dictionary
   recalls new words weekly

PUNCTUATION SKILLS:
1. Uses punctuation:
   periods
   capitals
   question marks
   commas
   quotation marks
   apostrophes
   exclamation points

BASIC READING SKILLS:
1. Reads on a daily basis:
   classmates names
   familiar class words
   own writing
   morning message
   teacher plans and memo
   independent library books
   science and social studies material (informational material)
2. Reads with comprehension at ____ level:
   understands main idea
   recognizes essential details
   understands vocabulary
   draws conclusions
   able to write about what has been read

COMMENTS:

No report card can ever replace direct contact between parent and teacher. At best, a good report form serves as a starting place for meaningful communication.

We believe letter grades, still used by all too many elementary schools, are counterproductive to student growth, self-esteem, and true parent understanding of children's developmental progress in school.

APPROACHES THAT WORK:
I Am Needed—
The Child as Tutor

"About the first day that I went to tutor I know four things. I was nervous a lot, scared a lot, excited a lot. After I tutored, I was happy, a whole lot."

The energy which children bring to tutoring is inspiring. The seriousness with which they approach their work is absolutely arresting, for tutoring is real work in a world which too often places little value on the offerings children are able to make. Adults are prone not only to do too much for children, but to ignore what children learn from each other.

- watch the quick steps of a child on the way to another classroom to tutor
- watch the openness and confidence with which two children in a tutoring relationship greet each other
- watch a tutor's body language as he struggles to clarify a point, to give another child the confidence to try
- watch the child being tutored: expectant, wanting to understand, silly, testing, serious, exuberant, awed

A developmental curriculum is built on an environment for learning in which the worth of the child is central, in which the child is loved and respected. It is based on a knowledge of child development which considers the social, emotional and physical development of the child as well as the intellectual. It is a natural setting for cross age activities in which children teach each other, in which children have genuine responsibilities and are held accountable for them.

When a child is asked to tutor another, you are saying to that child that she is needed and is an important person, that you believe that this child is capable of solving problems, of being responsible. Children have an urge to help and know when their efforts are taken seriously.

Beyond the burst of self-esteem, which is regularly buffeted and occasionally shattered by the reality of the frustrations of working with another person, are the myriad opportunities which the role of tutor presents to a child.

A five year old asks her tutor to tell the story of "The Three Bears" over and over again. The liveliness of the

Tutors take on a strong sense of responsibility and caring for the children they tutor.

tutor's rendition is very exciting. Bringing her playfulness and imagination to the story, she is as caught up in its rhythms as the child listening. "Next week," she says, "we could maybe act it out. Who would you like to be?"

Later that day the tutor records in her log the details of the session. "I had to tell 'The Three Bears' again. I'm getting good at it: first the porridge, then the chairs, then the beds. Susan likes my baby bear voice. I think I'm going to have to be all three bears again next week when we act it out. Susan wants to be Goldilocks."

At a tutor's seminar later that week she comments, "I wonder why Susan likes that story so much." Another tutor says, "I don't know, but my mother says we wore out three copies of *Rapunzel* when I was little." Another adds, "With the little boy I babysit, it's *Goodnight Moon*. You know that book? Goodnight moon, goodnight mouse, goodnight spoon." She shakes her head. "Those things are all dreamy—little kids are dreamy, spacey." (A very true point.) Someone comments on what a good idea it is to act the story out.

Another tutor, age 10, taps a soccerball lightly with the inside of her foot, passing it deftly to a ten year old a few feet away. "Try it." The child awkwardly imitates the tutor's sure motions. "That's it," the tutor encourges. "Do it again." The simple

lesson plans that this tutor prepares focus on introducing particular soccer skills one at a time. The child being tutored is becoming more comfortable with her body, more confident at recess.

The tutor knows that the child, Michelle, is new at the school, and has limited skills in sports. This and additional information was shared with her by the teacher in charge of the tutoring project. It is confidential information and she, the tutor, has shared it with none of her friends. The teacher had asked, "Do you think you could help Michelle? Would you like to help Michelle?" The tutor could and would. Michelle and the tutor are developing a special peer relationship that eases Michelle's transition to the school. Michelle seeks out her tutor in the lunchroom and tentatively sits beside her. Michelle's tutor chooses her to be on the A-team in gym. The tutor has observed her in the classroom. She is somewhat puzzled by the different aspects of Michelle's personality, but senses that Michelle really needs her.

Another tutor, age 11, laments to anyone who will listen, "How does that kid know what a googolplex is? I don't know what a googolplex is!! I'm supposed to be tutoring him!" The distinction between the tutor and the child being tutored blurs and disappears. The tutor is engaged in a delightful journey of discovery.

A child and his tutor look about thoughtfully and then with a giggle head for the darkest spot in the room—the closet. This isn't in the lesson plan, but six-year-old David is very excited about a penlight his aunt has given to him. Then his tutor has another idea. Seating himself on the floor, he opens his mouth wide and sticks out his tongue. "Yuck," says David, aiming the penlight at his mouth. "What is that wiggly thing?"

A 14-year-old tutor smacks her hand against her forehead in disbelief. "It's Tuesday! I'm so dumb. I'm tutoring today. I forgot my tutoring stuff at home." Her stomach churns. She draws upon all of her resources to calm herself and invents a hasty plan for tutoring time. If this were to become a pattern for the tutor, missing appointments with the child entrusted to her, forgetting her materials, balking at keeping a log, the teacher in charge of the tutoring project would sit down with the tutor and try to discover what was amiss, why the child was withdrawing from the role, endeavoring to salvage the tutoring relationship. If that were impossible, then the tutor and child would be guided in wrapping up the relationship, for not every child succeeds in the role of tutor. The 14-year-old tutor described above, however, is not in this situation. She has learned that she has greater resources than she thought and that she can depend upon herself in a crisis, but she will not forget her materials next week, and her tutor's log faithfully documents her momentary panic and the feeling in her stomach that accompanied it.

"All he wants to do is run around," complains a frustrated 12-year-old tutor. "I don't know what to do. How can I play the SORRY® game with him when he won't sit still? I give up. I thought this was gonna be fun. I don't understand. He didn't do that last week. I'm no good at this," and he slumps in his chair. These feelings pour forth in a tutor's seminar. "Let's try to figure out why Johnny's running around instead of playing with his tutor," says the teacher in charge of the seminar. "Maybe we could role play the situation first." Out of this session and many others on behavior and particularly on distractibility, will come insights into what makes children want to learn—what motivates them and what does not. The tutors discover by brainstorming techniques how to respond to these issues. It is the responsibility of the group to solve these problems with each other. The seminars are well prepared. They are to be taken seriously. They are actually teacher training, and the ongoing dialogue generated in them is critical to the success of the tutoring project. Topics discussed by the tutors have included direction giving, difficulties in implementing lesson plans, writing a record of their interactions in tutoring sessions, role playing and the areas of memory, visual learning and behavior. Some of the seminars are quite technical. Some of these tutors will later work with new tutors. They have much to learn about themselves and about understanding child behavior.

The teacher in charge of the tutoring project observes the tutoring session from time to time. "I like the way you spoke to David today. You were saying, 'Try again. How else can you do it? Will that work?' You are a good teacher, David." The teacher

has noticed over the years that those children who have been actively committed to tutoring and have truly taken on the responsibility for others, have also developed a sense of responsibility for the school community. The quality of their relationship with the school is somehow different. They are doing essential work, have been delegated real responsibilities, and because of this, the school has become their school.

A 13-year-old tutor listens patiently to Anna as she moves cautiously from word to word on her math instructions. The child looks up at her often. The tutor helps the child refocus on the next word. This is a difficult year for the tutor. The child will make very little progress. The tutor's expectations will not be met, cannot be met, and yet there is progress, but it is painfully slow. The tutor must be reassured often. Next year the tutor will need a break from the intensity and frustration of this particular relationship.

A child refuses to play a game of logic with her tutor. She shrugs her shoulders at the option of chess, rejects an excercise the tutor has prepared, and turns once more to the classroom shelf for the CONNECT FOUR® game. The 12-year-old tutor is perplexed by Sara. His understanding is that Sara is ahead of her class in math and that his time with her is really for math enrichment. He will bring this dilemma to the tutor's seminar. After much discussion another tutor will suggest that maybe this Sara has been pushed and pushed and just wants to play.

Thirteen-year-old Philip is a child with a very specific reading disability. His teacher taught him an approach to reading which works well as he

struggles to master this skill. Philip is now teaching this skill to another child. The validity of Philip as teacher is strengthened by the fact that he is overcoming a similar disability. Philip's understanding of what the child is going through is keen. His faith in the child's ability, unwavering.

The tutor's role is an exciting one. It stretches children, asks them to trust themselves, share themselves and risk themselves. They make decisions, make mistakes, try alternate methods, organize their time, explore their world in a new way, focus intently on another person's needs and in the process are confronted with themselves. But children who tutor must not be selected randomly. Not every child is ready to tutor; not every child can be tutored by another child. The needs of the child and the tutor must be balanced, and teachers, at every step of the way, must assume the ultimate responsibility for the tutoring project.

When the approach to tutoring in the classroom is a positive one, the child being tutored also feels special, important. And the child often responds favorably to the different pace, is often less fearful of making mistakes. The time that she spends with her tutor can be concentrated and charged with the remarkable sensitivity that one child can show for another.

There will be disappointments. "My tutor didn't come today. She didn't notice my new ring. He's crabby," and strong feelings, "I hate my tutor," but more often there is a spring in the step of a child who is saying, "That's my tutor," and particularly in the eyes of a younger child, awe, for balancing "I hate my tutor" is "I love my tutor."

Planning a Tutoring Program

A tutoring program in which *children* tutor can be an integral part of the developmental curriculum. If carefully planned, clearly understood by the children involved, guided with insight and appropriately monitored, a tutoring program can multiply the learning possibilities for children in every school.

Student tutoring is usually done by children in grades 5-8 who act as tutors in grades K-4. More familiar "peer" tutoring can also be included; however, our model primarily involves older children working with younger children. High school students also make excellent tutors. Such a program must have a teacher to initiate and guide the process—from selection of children to be tutored to recognition of the tutors who have participated at the end of the year. It would include:

- guidelines for choosing children to be tutored (They may be weak in a particular academic area, unskilled in sports, in need of social skills, making a transition to a new school, ready for more challenging work or have a very specific learning disability);

- guidelines for selecting tutors (The tutor must exhibit a readiness to take on the responsibility of working with another child, must have the skills required, differences in personalities must be assessed and paid attention to and the needs of the tutor balanced with the needs of the child);

- the creation of a tutor's seminar (Children tutoring have much to learn, many questions and a need for support. The teacher in charge of the seminar must be clear about what is expected of the tutors and the children being tutored. How are they to be with each other? What are their responsibilities? What are they to do when they can't handle a situation? How do they need to prepare? There must be firmness in dealing with such issues as irresponsible behavior, and strong praise when hurdles are overcome);

- documentation of the tutoring process (Contracts written between tutors and children being tutored, simple lesson plans for each session, logs in which tutors detail their feelings, strategies and observations);

- a plan for more experienced tutors to begin to work with beginning tutors;

- a plan to co-ordinate with other staff (When is tutoring to take place? How often for each child? Where will the tutor work? How will the children move between classrooms?); and

- specific schoolwide recognition of the role of tutors via an awards ceremony, certificates of achievement, banquet or other prominence.

Successful tutoring programs start small, with one teacher supervising no more than six tutors. Make sure the program is endorsed and supported by the administration and that tutoring is part of the tutor's regular academic program—not an extracurricular activity or "privilege" that means make-up work in regular classes. A tutoring program which follows these guidelines with children taking responsibility for their appointments, their preparation and their actions, allows children genuine responsibilities within a very clear and supportive structure.

The Developmental Curriculum Goes Home

And what about the parents...
frightened by your talk of Gesell
struggling with their doubts, risking their children
tentative in their understanding of Piaget
lost in the midst of your talk of curriculum?
Who will set the quiet, confident pace to draw them out?
Who will nurture, respect, ponder and observe them?
No doubt it could be you...You extending
the gift of time
the gift of patience
the gift of respect
Beyond the classroom walls.

Parent-teacher relationships are important to the success of a developmental curriculum. A staff which espouses the developmental approach must be prepared to make a commitment of time, energy and purpose with parents which generally exceeds that ordinarily proferred. If parent relations are made a low priority or parents are continually viewed as audience rather than as participants in the classroom drama, then the future of a developmental approach is in jeopardy.

Parent-teacher relationships are difficult to develop. They take an extraordinary amount of insight and care. They call for balance, wit and patience. And often because there is so much to tend to, we let a gap between ourselves and parents form, widen and become filled with uncomfortable tensions.

We find ourselves reacting angrily to the parent who has little understanding of our classroom goals, when we ourselves did not take the time to communicate them clearly; reacting with disbelief to the parent who has never visited our classroom and is shocked to hear that her daughter is playing with blocks at age seven, when we didn't take the time to explain that blocks are an integral piece of our program; reacting with frustration to the parent who is not excited about our curriculum, when we haven't thought to send home a picture of her child totally involved in building an access ramp to a three-story garage, or invited a parent to visit the classroom "museum of houses."

If we somehow manage to navigate these obstacles, and do communicate with a great sense of purpose all of this information, there is absolutely no guarantee that a parent will understand or react appropriately. All too often a parent's doubts and anxieties outstrip his intuitions that the developmental path is valid. And then we react with pain. A parent does not accept a child's developmental placement, questions, waffles, gives in at a time when he needs to stand firm, and we are unprepared for the intensity of our emotions. We are defensive when we should advocate positively and professionally for our point of view.

When communication breaks down, it is our job to bridge the gap. How is it that a parent has stormed into the principal's office and refuses to let her child participate in a field trip? How is it that a parent is driven to pit his child against his teacher? How is it that a parent sets about undermining the credibility of a teacher among other parents?

We need to acknowledge how poorly prepared many of us are to deal with these problems. We have no plan and sometimes work at cross-purposes.

We need to recognize that some of our basic tenets about parents ("Life would be simpler without them," for example) are the seeds of mistrust. This recognition is essential to the process of sorting out just how important parents are as co-operative partners within our curriculum, how essential their confidence and trust are to the success of a developmental approach.

Parents are teachers too. Their understanding of how they can function in relation to their children and the learning process is crucial.

The relationship between the child and teacher in the developmental classroom is different. It speaks of a conviction about what is good for a child. It speaks of a child's worthiness and a teacher's compatibility with the child's rhythm. If this difference is grasped by parents, it can be built upon at home. The intuition of many parents affirms that a developmental curriculum is somehow right for their children, but in order to articulate this "rightness," to act upon it, they need help and guidance. We must observe, ponder, respect and nurture our parents who are struggling with these doubts, doubts which are stronger than their intuitions.

One of the most helpful beginnings is a simple exercise which defines and clarifies teacher relationships with parents. This exercise acknowledges that parents are important, that we must plan for parents with the care that we plan for their children, that the communication about the content of our program and its specific goals must be concrete, must be as meticulously orchestrated as our classroom environment.

Defining the Parent-Teacher Relationship

To begin, you will need to write out the answers to the following questions:

1. What is one thing you want parents to understand about the developmental approach?
2. What is it that you wish parents would be excited about in your curriculum?
3. How do you wish parents to participate in your classroom?
4. What do you want the tone of your relationship with parents to be?

A teacher in a school using a developmental curriculum answered these questions in the following way, developing a profile of the parent-teacher relationship. Compare your answers to his.

"What is one thing you want parents to understand about the developmental approach?"
There are actually two things I would like parents to know about the developmental approach:

FIRST—there is no relationship between development and intelligence. When we recommend extra time for a child in school, a parent's first reaction is often that of failure—their failure, their child's failure. "What did I do wrong?" they ask. Or, "Is my child stupid?"

We are not "keeping a child back" as parents remember it from their school days, but rather providing a gift of time so children can respond to their own timetables. This notion is one of the hardest for parents to understand and certainly the most important.

SECOND—I would like parents to view their child's education as a continuum that takes many years. If I am a first grade teacher, I do not expect the child's reading ability to be complete; if I am a fourth grade teacher, I do not expect multiplication tables to be internalized. I want parents to appreciate the learning process as a growth process. I want them to see that we are not in the fast food business—that we cannot produce instant results.

"What is it that you wish parents would be excited about in your curriculum?"
This is a hard question. Parents are most often excited by their children's products, the tangible finished work they can see. It is difficult for them to see the child's process—how they got to that product—but that's what I'd like them to be excited about. My job is to figure out how to share that process with them. As a teacher I can watch a child work for a week revising a piece of writing, or glueing miniature houses on a map. I can glow with pride over their perseverance and growing competence the way a parent will, watching his child in the final production of the class

play. I guess my responsibility is to find a way to share all of the rehearsals with parents.

"How do you wish parents to participate in your classroom?"
I love to have parents as volunteers in the classroom when they are willing to contribute and take a specific responsibility. Sometimes it's easier if the parents aren't parents of children in your class. The best volunteer I ever had, Mrs. O'Malley, came twice a week with her knitting and could fit into anything we were doing. I really didn't have to prepare for her much and I guess that's important too. She was at ease with us whether we were having a good day or a bad day and she understood and appreciated that sometimes we have bad days. If we were reading a story when she arrived, her knitters would join her quietly in a corner of the meeting rug and work silently. If we were finishing up a science project, she would wait or help her knitters clean up. And she talked to me! She let me know how she felt about the kids, and asked questions about behavior she didn't understand. She followed our room rules and school rules exactly and didn't try to impose her own. Her personality was enough. The children loved her and learned from her. When she moved away, there was an emptiness on Tuesdays and Thursdays.

"What do you want the tone of your relationship with parents to be?"
Trust. Mutual trust. When parents and I feel that special trust; when we understand we both are doing the best we can to help the child grow and thrive, then there is a relaxed and warm relationship between home and school. In such a relationship the child is nurtured and supported. The child, perceiving this interaction

between her parents and her teacher feels surrounded by love and concern. This is the environment we seek for each child.

Now put yourself in the parent's shoes and walk through the school year in your mind. How would you answer the following questions? Write down your answers.

1. What would make you more comfortable about school?
2. What do you need to know?
3. How do you want the teacher to communicate with you?
4. If your child were a student in this classroom, how would you know he was having a successful year?

Answers that parents have given to these questions include the following: Compare them to your answers.

1. I will be comfortable if I know that the classroom is a safe, supportive place for my child.
2. I need to know very specifically what your goals are as a teacher in specific areas and where my child fits in the midst of these. I need to know that you as a teacher are competent and confident.
3. I want you as a teacher to respect me, to include me.
4. I want reports and conferences to be concrete, to expand my knowledge of my child. I want to know—to deepen my experience of who my child is.

Once you have defined the parent-teacher realtionship as clearly as you can, delineating carefully your expectations and their needs, you will be ready to work toward that relationship in very specific ways. Here are some possibilities to help you begin.

1. WAYS TO HELP PARENTS UNDERSTAND THE DEVELOPMENTAL APPROACH:
   - Plan a parents' night during which parents participate in activities their children have undertaken.
   - Write notes on planning sheets which children complete daily (see pages 48-49 for form).
   - In your first conference, specify areas you and the child are working on.
   - Share written evaluations which specify group goals as well as individual goals, with comments about the specific child.
   - Lend books and background material to parents which will help them to understand your classroom approach. Design a booklet which answers questions which your parents frequently ask, and discuss it at the beginning of the school year.

2. WAYS TO HELP PARENTS
   BECOME EXCITED ABOUT YOUR
   CURRICULUM:
   • Share a slideshow of a typical
     day in your classroom.
   • Telephone to invite a parent
     to see a block structure or other
     project a child has worked
     hard on.
   • Send a photo of a child at work
     in the classroom to a parent who
     can't/doesn't/won't come to the
     school.
   • Have children write invitations
     to parents to see the classroom
     "museum of houses," play, art
     show, publishing center, block
     village.
   • Prepare (with children) a weekly,
     biweekly, or monthly bulletin
     which shares some of the class-
     room events and excitement.
3. WAYS TO ENCOURAGE
   PARENTS TO PARTICIPATE IN
   THE CLASSROOM:
   • Compile a list of skills parents
     would like to share and skills
     they would like to learn; use it.
   • Don't give up. If one approach
     doesn't reach a parent, try
     another.
   • Have a child act as a guide for
     parents volunteering in the
     classroom.
4. WAYS TO AFFECT THE TONE OF
   YOUR PARENT RELATIONSHIPS:
   • Call home when a child's
     behavior is puzzling, unusual.
   • Pay particular attention to the
     child's circumstances in single-
     parent families.
   • Hold a three-way conference
     before school begins in which
     parent/child/teacher share some
     of their hopes for the school year
   • Administer parent contact in
     small, frequent doses.
   • Follow up on parents' notes.
     Write the reply on the note and
     xerox a copy for the file.
   • Respect the families' culture/
     heritage/traditions/values by
     handling personal information
     discreetly.
   • Remember, if a relationship
     with a parent is not healthy, you
     can work together to change it.
     Know what you are working on
     and what your goals are.
   • Help a parent find out how
     much she knows about a child:
     "What is your child's favorite
     color, book, food, television pro-
     gram, activity, etc.? Who is your
     child's favorite person?"
   • Meet with parents specifically
     to share information, to solve a
     problem, to brainstorm.

Monitoring Your Progress

When we undertake a specific
plan for working with parents, we
need to know whether or not it is
working. A chart with benchmarks or
a file card for each parent will help:

Smiths conf. 9/4 note 9/18 helped w/field trip 9/24

Ryans unable to conf. note 9/10 missed open house

Streamline the system, checking it
from time to time to see that whole
clumps of parents are not being overlooked, that you are not focusing all
of your energies on a small, articulate
or vocal group.

The teacher who can anticipate
parent anxieties, who can "read"
parents well, who is confident enough
to focus on the parents' needs, and
respond to what a parent does not
say, will become a parent-nurturing
teacher. Encourage parents to express
their doubts, to ask their questions
and be willing to solve a problem with
a parent. Trust will be the result.

What Did You Do in School Today?

A translation for parents

"I played. I made a doggie out of clay. I strung beads on a string. I did a finger-puppet thing."

Using the small muscles of the fingers and hand in a variety of purposeful activities fosters the dexterity necessary for good handwriting control. Today your kindergartener may have also practiced printing alphabet letters or numbers on paper. You are less likely to hear about this activity.

"I played. I made a picture of a truck. I played duck, duck goose. I got to use the wagon and I built a castle in the blocks."

The control of the large muscles of the shoulders, arms and legs help improve general bodily co-ordination. This co-ordination is necessary to further development of spatial awareness, organizational and patterning skills required for math, reading and appropriate social skills.

"I played house and baked a cake. Teacher wrote a story about our walk. We sang a new song today. I'll teach it to you."

Language development is the foundation for competent and creative reading and writing skills. A strong language storehouse is built in the brain through direct experience translated by the teacher orally and visually. The more language patterns available to the child *prior* to formal reading instruction, the better reader that child will be.

"I played in the blocks. Billy made a garage, but it was too big so I made a ramp. Suzie made a sign to show IN and OUT. We got to drive cars and park 'em in our garage."

Blocks in kindergarten and the primary grades are used to teach mathematical concepts and social skills. A garage and its ramp yield understanding of proportion. A simple question from the teacher can teach fractions ½, ¼. Children measure, count and compute real problems from their block structures, often doing it co-operatively, just as they do their constructions.

"I played in the sand table. There were beans in it! My cup had more beans cause it was higher, but Mary said she had more cause hers was fatter."

What goes on at a sand table in kindergarten is much different than in nursery school. A variety of measuring devices yields comparisons and active thinking about size, volume, equalities. Fractions are again available to the teacher in a highly concrete form. Social learning and co-operative working continue to be enhanced.

"We cooked. We made dough and shaped it out. It was fun."

Today the children made the letters of their names in playdough with cookie cutters. The teacher will take them home and bake them tonight. Soon they will be made into beautiful signboards that some day will come home as presents. Until then the children can copy the letters onto paper, practicing letter formation over and over in a natural way.

"I just played and did nothin."

Some days are like that. Not every moment of every school day is memorable or productive. However, there may be more behind this common statement than meets the ear. It may have been one of the best learning days of all, so filled with different activities and events they are too many to recount right away. Be patient, don't probe and insist on a blow-by-blow account of each day. You're liable to learn more if you wait.

"I did my work. I did my papers. Here."

Do expect *some* papers home in kindergarten and the primary grades. Paintings, writings and math work belong on the front of your refrigerator. But be alert if your child brings home only purple dittos with happy faces and talks only about his work. Seat work in workbooks and dittos may not be all that's being done, but it would be good to find out how much. A healthy balance between experience and reinforcement is the goal of a good elementary teacher.

A REFLECTION:
When a Teacher Looks Inside

My name is Jay Lord. I am a teacher.

I have strong memories of my first assignment in a big public high school in Washington, D.C.—a school of three thousand young people perched on a slight rise in the middle of one of the poorest areas of our capital. I was young, inexperienced and somewhat afraid. I reported to work a day before school began to attend the first staff meeting of the year. After several long corridors, I found the auditorium, took my seat and sighed through the humidity that hangs so close on a later summer day in Washington. The meeting complete, I started to wander back to my room, 221, only to suddenly realize that I was hopelessly and utterly lost—that I had no idea how to negotiate this huge building, and even less of an idea how I would face a homeroom and five sophomore English classes the next day.

When I look back upon those first years, I realize how little I knew and how quickly I went to work to establish both distance and order in my students. I wanted them to know that I was in charge, that I was not their contemporary, and most of all, I wanted not to deal with my total lack of knowledge about them.

The tool that I used to achieve these ends was my many and varied, some quite ingenious, curriculum plans. I would labor far into the night, night after night, relearning aspects of formal grammar, creating spelling lists, reading through the poets, struggling with decisions about research paper design and wondering which of the great books I knew well enough to teach. I had the head of the English Department to help me, and a principal who often visited unannounced to notice both the order of the room and the hole in the sole of my shoe. A big black notebook remained perched on my desk, filling slowing with the daily lesson plans, one for each day and one for each of the tenth grade classes. Slowly a library grew in my room filled with dictionaries, thesauruses and poems that were missing so blatantly in the rest of the school. And as a young, single man experiencing a big city for the first time in my life, I had to put away my social life for the mass of papers that passed across my desk each night. My red pencil became somewhat permanently attached to my left hand as I noted time after time, night after night: "A sentence begins with a capital; subject and verb must agree; please enter this word in your spelling book; have you ever heard of a period?" Days when I felt better about myself my red pencil gained more sophistication, it would go into footnotes, points of logic and an occasional discussion of an idea.

That first year passed slowly, I gained confidence, my kids did start to write poetry, but there was no noticeable upswing in their ability to write. My job became easier as I became more and more comfortable with my red pencil. I also discovered the power of worksheets for those days when the children needed to practice or I had come up blank the night before or there was simply too much confusion in the room. I discovered in a little bookshop on the corner of K and 16th Street, a wealth of reproducible worksheets that took kids through the beginning steps of writing. I still remember the utter sense of safety that I felt when it became known to me that this type of curriculum work had been done. There was a clear, discernible sigh as I realized that my nightly journey into curriculum development could be relaxed, that much of my job I could let go of when I needed to and turn it over to these reproducible worksheets. In fact, the principal, Mr. Kaighn, a stern, warm man, came into my room on one of those Monday mornings when I had been traveling all weekend, to discover my use of these patterned writing worksheets. He felt moved to send me a note the next day on how nicely I was adjusting. Mrs. Field, the head of the English Department, visited soon after and was also impressed except for my constant use of the word stuff.

The year wound down. I found out for the first time the beauty of snow—it creates snow days; I learned to smoke in a closeted teacher's room where I ran for my free period—five cigarettes long; I learned my way around the building; I started on my second black notebook, leaving the first full and untouched on its assigned place on my desk in the front of the room just in front of the blackboard. My room had books, a postered corner and a fair number of supplies which I had wheedled and bargained for in a very poor school. By March, I had even managed to get a seat for everyone of my students and the cutting seemed down. My rule that you automatically failed if you cut more than three times a

semester was firm, fair and had been used when necessary. Even Roger Lewis, the most recalcitrant of all of my students, was attending class. I felt moderately proud of my growth as a teacher, and even on trips home, carried myself quite straight in my knowledge that I was teaching in one of the hardest high schools in D.C. and that I was making it.

One day, when I did not want to be in school, when I was filled with images of North Truro where I would soon be vacationing; when I could literally hear the surf and feel the power of the waves as I swept to shore, riding a foamy white crest, I started to take note of a somewhat disquieting pattern that I was beginning to develop. In the name of efficiency, I was starting to lump all of my tenth grade English classes together. When I did this it meant that five times a day, I went over the same material, in the same order, using the same examples. It was clear to me that by my fifth presentation of the day I had honed my material and delivery into an effective piece; and that, I could, through this clumping, come much more prepared for class with a much fuller knowledge of the material because I was focusing on one point— on one progression in the clear curriculum path that I was following.

On this day, immersed in my third straight presentation of the same material, I suddenly lost my place. I was in front of the class, I had chalk in my hand, I was writing on the board, a wave broke on the Truro beach, and I lost what I was saying, what I was writing, and where I was. I stood quietly, staring out at the thirty-four young faces waiting and I wasn't sure what I was doing.

I held my tongue for once. I didn't go hide. I stared slowly at the children that I had been talking to.

Mary Washington, her books piled neatly on the corner of her desk; Roger Lewis, a tall afro rising above blazing brown eyes; 300 pound Rachel squeezed into her desk; Gregory in his eternal slouch—all watching, dependent on me to go on, stuck without my words, filling their pages with the writing on the board, waiting for the information I would bring them. I looked back at the board and found Robert Frost waiting. I found the long stone fences separating good neighbors, birches that bent and a little horse that would think it queer to stop. I stood between the board and the children, behind my desk—between the riches of Georgetown and the poverty of Southeast, behind position—between my world and theirs, behind curriculum. I was the court jester. the magic man, the policemen and the

intellectual passing the country to the city, white to black, adult to youth, the formal to the idiom, the society to the individual, the past to the future. I was bringing to the children, acting on them, writing all over them with my chalk. What sense could a 14 year old with a key around his neck who had never been out of Southeast Washington make of a birch tree— what is a stone wall if it is not those brick walls so carefully constructed throughout Washington, to keep them out—and a horse? I had missed the point.

"Hey, Mr. Lord." I moved gingerly from behind my desk.

"Yes?"

"I never seen a birch tree."

"Oh, I think you have—Robert Frost lived throughout Vermont and found images that were universal— the birch tree as our soul—swaying in the breeze—bending with the weight of snow, burden, but not breaking because it bent—able to rise to the spring sun once the snow was gone. It is in sense a type of rebirth—revelation."

"Is that a birch tree?"

"I never seen a tree bend," Gregory sat up.

"Yea, man, I go by that tree every day on 13th Street—it's never bent."

"No, a birch tree is slender, covered with a thin, white, smooth bark. You can peel it right off the tree. Birches have thousands of small, slender branches that catch snow, hold the snow on a cold day, bending the tree with the weight of the piled snow. It's beautiful, the white snow against the white bark, bent."

"How come everything's white?"

"I got on my white hat; I'm the good guy."

"No, trees have rough coats, ain't you ever seen a dog scratch up against one."

"Anyway, snow ain't white—it's dirty—it's kind of chocolate colored on the street."

"Yea, and it never snows that much, how could it pile up?"

"Sides, I never seen a tree that had many leaves in the winter—they just stand there next to the poles with the wires."

"Wait, slow down Gregory. Please. Robert Frost lived most of his life in New England. He lived in the country where there are acres and acres of forested land dotted with clumps of those birch trees. You almost always find them together, they seed each other, they sway together. There is a kind of restfulness that comes from being lost in the gentle sway of the trees when a breeze stirs them— white on green—waving."

"I wonder if they got black trees with blood red leaves?"

"They don't grown together. Even in Lincoln Park, they only got ten— twelve trees."

"And they got wire wrapped around them."

"How come that wires on the trees?"

"How come dogs pee on trees? You ever seen that big, black doberman in behind the school. He's bad. Walking around, peeing everywhere."

The class broke up. Rachel stood up, twisted to find Roger's laughing eyes. Gregory sat up, reaching forward, whispering to Mary. I was on the edge of the desk. The class was alive—it was loud—there was movement. They had taken over from me. I was watching as conversation shot back and forth. Robert Frost was lost. The birch trees were gone. I tried to quiet the class but I couldn't.

The bell rang, pulling the kids back, books gather—I erased the board, sat at my desk, stunned, filled with questions, longing for ways to know these children, knowing that I had seen them for the first time, not knowing what I had seen, feeling bent, filled with revelation.

The students are younger—I am older. I am no longer teaching at a big inner city high school; but, rather a small independent lab school, the Greenfield Center School. My classroom balances what I know about children, their developmental stages, with what I know about those questions that they so often raise. My black notebook is still on my desk, now filled with daily observations of children at their work.

General Developmental Theory

APPRENTICESHIP IN THINKING: COGNITIVE DEVELOPMENT IN SOCIAL CONTEXT. Barbara Rogoff. New York/Oxford: Oxford University Press, 1990.

This important theoretical work explains the view that the greatest cognitive growth occurs through social interaction. Based on the work of Vygotsky and others, Rogoff details her own careful study of teaching and learning through "guided participation" in several different cultures. Impressive theory to support both the social curriculum and developmentally appropriate practice.

ARNOLD GESELL. THEMES OF HIS WORK. Louise Bates Ames. New York: Human Sciences Press. 1989.

This is the definitive work on Gesell's career and contribution to the field of child development written by his respected colleague. An exceptional summary with glimpses into Gesell's connections with Piaget, Mead and others.

CHILD BEHAVIOR. Frances L. Ilg, M.D., Louise Bates Ames, Ph.D., Sidney M. Baker, M.D. Revised Edition. New York: Harper & Row, 1981.

Originally published in 1955, *Child Behavior* is one of the classic "handbooks" for parents. It contains the basic developmental theory Dr. Arnold Gesell pioneered from 1915-1950 at Yale University. Specific information on normal behavior for children between birth and age sixteen is put forth for all areas of daily life. A new section by Dr. Baker examines the role of health in overall development.

CHILDHOOD AND SOCIETY. Erik H. Erikson. New York: W.W. Norton & Co., Inc., 1963. (Revised Edition)

Erikson's stage theory of psycho-social growth and development is detailed in one long chapter in this book. While this theory is available elsewhere, this book provides the source material.

COMPARING THEORIES OF CHILD DEVELOPMENT. R. Murray Thomas. Belmont, CA: Wadsworth Publishing Co., 1979.

A scholarly effort comparing theories, and models with an evaluation built into each chapter. College level reading or above. Major considerations given to Gesell, Lewin, Werner, Freud, Erikson, Piaget, Vygotsky, Kohlberg, Skinner, Maslow & Buhler. Applied theories of Montessori, Durkin, Kephart and Koppitz are also given a chapter.

A good annotated bibliography.

THEORIES OF DEVELOPMENT: CONCEPTS AND APPLICATIONS. William C. Crain. Englewood Cliffs, NJ: Prentice-Hall, Inc. 1980.

For basic background and historical perspective of the most important figures in child development and psychology, this is a wonderful survey. Chapter 1 covers Locke, Rousseau and other early theories; Chapter 2 evaluates Gesell's maturational theory; and the following 14 chapters deal with one or more significant theoriticians including: Darwin, Lorenz, Montessori, Piaget, Kohlberg, Freud, Erikson, Bettelheim, Jung, Pavlov, Watson and Skinner.

A very readable introductory text, suitable for student and lay person alike; yet not at all shallow in its treatment.

WHAT ARE SCHOOLS FOR? HOLISTIC EDUCATION IN AMERICAN CULTURE. Ron Miller. Brandon, VT: Holistic Education Press, 1990.

Ron Miller is the Editor of *Holistic Education Review*, perhaps the most insightful educational journal available to teachers today. This book is a thorough and perceptive historical treatment of American education. Puts today's trends in perspective.

The Popular Press

EDUCATING FOR CHARACTER: HOW OUR SCHOOLS CAN TEACH RESPECT AND RESPONSIBILITY. Thomas Lickona. New York: Bantam Books, 1991. Available through Northeast Foundation for Children, Greenfield, MA.

From the author of *Raising Good Children*, this book faces the controversial issue of "values education." Lickona cuts through the controversy to spotlight dozens of successful programs which teach values necessary for our children's moral development. He presents a 12-point program of practical strategies for creating a working coalition of parents, teachers, and communities, and discusses the educator as a role model, the classroom as a moral community, and patterns of positive discipline.

THE HURRIED CHILD: GROWING UP TOO FAST TOO SOON (Revised Edition). David Elkind. Reading, MA: Addison Wesley, 1988.

David Elkind is a noted Piagetian scholar who turns his attention to a sociological treatment of developmental theory. Provocative, if uneven.

Other books by Elkind include *All Grown-up and No Place to Go: Teenagers in Crisis* and *Miseducation: Preschoolers at Risk*.

VOICES FROM THE INSIDE: A REPORT ON SCHOOLING FROM INSIDE THE CLASSROOM. The Institute for Education in Transformation at the Claremont Graduate School. Claremont, CA: Claremont Graduate School, 1992. Available through Northeast Foundation for Children, Greenfield, MA.

This 18-month study discusses its methods and findings and identifies seven issues which the authors believe schools must address before creating meaningful change: (1) relationships, (2) race, culture, and class, (3) values, (4) teaching and learning, (5) safety, (6) physical environment, (7) despair, hope, and the process of change. Summaries are available in Spanish, Chinese, and Vietnamese.

YOUR TEN-TO-FOURTEEN-YEAR-OLD. Louise Bates Ames, Frances L. Ilg and Sidney M. Baker. New York: Delacorte Press, 1988.

This is the most recent book in the highly successful series from the Gesell Institute of Human Development. With humor and wisdom, this insightful study helps unlock the secrets of adolescence, and offers advice on how to make this time of enormous change less stressful and infinitely more enjoyable for everyone - the adolescent, the family and the school community.

Based on firsthand studies of adolescents, it traces the development of behavior (physical, psychological, emotional, interpersonal and ethical) in the home, school and community. It offers examples and analyses of these stages and puts them in perspective. Parents will find this book a source of encouragement, understanding and guidance.

YOUR TWO YEAR OLD. Louise Bates Ames. New York: Delacorte Press, 1979.

A delightful series of paperbacks which includes *Your One Year Old* through *Your Eight Year Old* (in separate volumes). Gesell Institute philosophy and practical advice regarding routines, interests and abilities for each age. Excellent references for parents.

Social Curriculum: Home and School

BETWEEN PARENT AND CHILD. Dr. Haim Ginott. New York, NY: Avon, 1969.

First published in 1956, this book is a classic in the field of child psychology, child development and parent guidance. Dr. Ginott was one of the first psychologists to translate an "enlightened" understanding of children into practical, easily understood principles and methods "to guide parents in living with children in mutual respect and dignity." The book offers "concrete suggestions and preferred solutions for dealing with daily situations and psychological problems faced by all parents."

CARING: A FEMININE APPROACH TO ETHICS AND MORAL EDUCATION. Nel Noddings. Berkeley: University of California Press, 1984.

Buy this book and read chapter eight. It will fire your imagination and desire to work for change in your school.

CARING TO LEARN: THE POSITIVE INPACT OF A SOCIAL CURRICULUM. Stephen N. Elliott. Greenfield, MA: Northeast Foundation for Children, 1993.

This research study assesses academic performance, social skills and problem behavior at Savin Rock Elementary School in West Haven, CT, at two points: before and after implementation of a social curriculum in the 3rd, 4th and 5th grade classrooms. The study solicited input from 200 students, their parents and teachers, and from participants at two control schools.

Conclusions include increases in social skills and decreases in problem behaviors, greater gains in behavior for students with educational handicaps and African American students, and improved home-school communication and understanding of social skills.

Elliott is a coauthor of the *Social Skills Rating system* and the *Social Skills Intervention Guide.*

CHILDREN: THE CHALLENGE. Rudolf Dreikurs, M.D. with Vicki Soltz, R.N. New York: E.P. Dutton, 1987.

First published in 1964 this classic by one of America's foremost psychiatrists lays the foundation for understanding and dealing with children's behavior and misbehavior. Through real-life anecdotes, Dreikurs shares how adults can apply this understanding to create positive interactions with children, to cope with their daily problems, and to maintain discipline humanely and with mutual respect. Very readable and eminently practical.

THE COOPERATIVE SPORTS AND GAMES BOOK. Terry Orlick. New York: Pantheon Books, 1978. Available through Northeast Foundation for Children, Greenfield, MA.

Orlick describes an approach to play and games that is based on cooperation, not competition. He presents over one hundred new games that "have been created, selected, and refined so that children can have fun while learning positive things about themselves, about others and about how they should behave in the world." Includes a good bibliography.

DESIGNING GROUPWORK: STRATEGIES FOR THE HETEROGENEOUS CLASSROOM. Elizabeth G. Cohen. New York: Teachers College Press, 1986.

This book explores how children can more actively contribute, share, and learn from an approach to teaching that includes groupwork. Groupwork can help to create a classroom where children truly listen to one another and express a mutual respect. Cohen discusses the advantages and dilemmas of groupwork, its use in multi-ability and bilingual classrooms, and step-by-step approaches to successful planning, implementation and evaluation of groupwork activities.

DISCIPLINE WITHOUT TEARS. Rudolph Dreikurs and Pearl Cassel. New York: Dutton, 1972.

Contains the basic Dreikurs approach to discipline which underlies so much of good classroom management practice. Not to be taken literally, but extremely useful for teachers digging deeply into their understanding of behavior.

EVERYONE WINS: COOPERATIVE GAMES AND ACTIVITIES. Sambhava and Josette Luvmour. Philadelphia, PA: New Society Publishers, 1990.

This is an easy to use, quick reference guide packed with over 150 cooperative games and activities that are developmentally graded according to appropriate age level, activity level, group size and location. These games can help children resolve conflict, enhance communication, build self-esteem, appreciate nature, laugh with each other, be creative, and have fun!

THE FRIENDLY CLASSROOM FOR A SMALL PLANET. Prutzman, Stern, Burger and Bodenhamer. Philadelphia, PA: New Society Publishers, 1988. Available through Northeast Foundation for Children, Greenfield, MA.

This is an essential sourcebook for any teacher, parent or adult leader trying to create a cooperative and supportive learning environment for children. It is based on the Children's Creative Response to Conflict Program which developed an approach to teaching cooperation and conflict resolution using puppetry, games, music and discussion. It serves as both a training manual and resource book for those interested in CCRC's approach.

The approach is divided into themes focused on communication, cooperation, affirmation and conflict resolution. A comprehensive bibliography is included.

HOW TO TALK SO KIDS WILL LISTEN & LISTEN SO KIDS WILL TALK. Adele Faber and Elaine Mazlish. New York: Avon, 1980. Available through Northeast Foundation for Children, Greenfield, MA.

This book gives parents and teachers a practical guide to learning the kind of communication with children that will "affirm the dignity and humanity of both." Based on the work of the late Dr. Haim Ginott, the authors' supportive and effective methods teach adults how to gain children's true cooperation, really understand and deal with children's concerns and feelings, find alternatives to punishment, and build children's self-esteem.

Other books on this topic by Faber and Mazlish include *Liberated Parents, Liberated Children* (Avon, 1974) and *Siblings Without Rivalry* (Avon, 1987).

KEEPING THE PEACE. Susanne Wichert. Philadelphia, PA: New Society Publishers, 1989. Available through Northeast Foundation for Children, Greenfield, MA.

Although written with preschoolers in mind, it provides a clear philosophy and excellent practical applications for teaching children cooperation, care, and creative conflict resolution that are entirely appropriate for children through 3rd grade. Wichert uses concrete, detailed examples to examine how the physical environment, teacher language, and the level and kind of teacher intervention affect children's ability to learn and practice cooperative ways of solving social problems.

Includes an extensive list of games and exercises which can help build a foundation of friendliness, care, and cooperation.

A MOVING EXPERIENCE. Teresa Benzwie. Tucson, AZ: Zephyr Press, 1987. Available through Northeast Foundation for Children, Greenfield, MA.

Benzwie provides a practical, step-by-step guide to integrating all areas of the curriculum — from math to art — through movement, dance, music and games. No experience in movement is necessary. The approach encourages children to develop high self-esteem and positive values, and to respect and support one another as they explore creative movement. An extensive listing of music selections and a well-developed bibliography are included.

POSITIVE DISCIPLINE. Jane Nelsen. New York: Ballantine, 1987.

Based on the work of Rudolf Dreikurs, this book gives a practical, step-by-step guide to home and school discipline using principles of encouragement, kindness and mutual respect. Describing real-life home and classroom situations, Jane Nelsen, psychologist and educator, provides parents and teachers with effective tools for helping children learn to be responsible for their own behavior.

THE SECOND COOPERATIVE SPORTS AND GAMES BOOK. Terry Orlick. New York: Pantheon Books, 1982. Available through Northeast Foundation for Children, Greenfield, MA.

With over 200 new, active, indoor and outdoor games for players of all ages, sizes and abilities, this is not a repetition of Orlick's popular first book. But the philosophy remains the same — "when people play together and not against each other, they have more fun."

TEACHING CHILDREN SELF-DISCIPLINE AT HOME AND AT SCHOOL. Thomas Gordon, New York: Random House, 1989,

From the originator of Parent Effectiveness Training and Teacher Effectiveness Training comes this new volume of value to both parents and teachers.

TEACHING CHILDREN TO CARE. Ruth S. Charney. Greenfield, MA: Northeast Foundation for Children, 1992.

Charney proposes that teaching ethical behavior is as important as teaching the 3 R's, and that caring and community can be taught in every classroom. She provides theory, guidelines for getting started, and narrative examples.

The first six weeks of school are used to lay the foundation for an ongoing social curriculum which can then be integrated throughout the year with a variety of related skills and techniques.

In a final section, "Clear Positives," Charney emphasizes the usefulness of self-reflection for teachers and describes how they can translate their own basic values in teaching

into classroom goals. It is a book founded on the day-to-day realities of teaching and provides vivid examples which every teacher can recognize.

YOU CAN'T SAY YOU CAN'T PLAY. Vivian Gussin Paley. Cambridge, MA: Harvard University Press, 1992.

Paley employs a unique strategy to probe the moral dimensions of the classroom. She departs from her previous work by extending her analysis to children through the 5th grade, all the while weaving remarkable fairy tales into her narrative description.

Paley introduces a new rule — "You can't say you can't play" — to her kindergarten classroom and solicits the opinions of older children regarding the fairness of such a rule. We hear from those who are rejected a well as those who do the rejecting. This book speaks to some of our most deeply held beliefs. Is exclusivity part of human nature? Can we legislate fairness and still nurture creativity and individuality? Paley leads us to some answers by listening to her children.

Other books by Paley include *The Boy Who Would Be a Helicopter: The Uses of Storytelling in the Classroom* (Harvard, 1990) and *Wally's Stories: Conversations in the Kindergarten* (Harvard, 1981).

Development in the Classroom

THE COGNITIVELY ORIENTED CURRICULUM/ HIGH SCOPE EDUCATIONAL RESEARCH FOUNDATION. Ypsilanti, MI: The High Scope Press.

There are dozens of publications, curriculum guides, films and related materials produced by the Foundation that are of immense significance for anyone interested in implementing some aspects of developmental curriculum.

Based on nearly 15 years of research and classroom activity, *The Cognitively Oriented Curriculum* is clearly among the best available material for teachers in this field. Send for a free catalog from the Foundation.

Among the most important works (particularly for teachers) are: *Young Children in Action: A Manual for Preschool Educators.* Mary Hohmann, Bernard Banet and David P. Weikart. Ypsilanti, MI: The High Scope Press, 1979. *The Cognitively Oriented Curriculum* (Elementary Education Series). Various authors, includes curricula on writing, reading, sewing, planning by teachers, etc. Films: "The Cognitively Oriented Curriculum; A Framework for Education." 19 minutes. "Thinking and Reasoning in Preschool Children." 23 minutes. "The Daily Routine." 30 minutes. Send for Audio-Visual Catalog, High Scope Press, 600 North River St., Ypsilanti, MI 48197. Monographs: "The Ypsilanti Perry Preschool Project: Preschool Years and Longitudinal Results through Fourth Grade." Weikart, Bond, and NcNeil. 1978. (Among other monographs, stands out as "proof" of the value of early intervention and developmental classrooms.)

CONSTRUCTIVE PLAY: APPLYING PAIGET IN THE PRESCHOOL. George Forman and Fleet Hill. Belmont, CA: Brooks/Cole Publishing Company, 1980.

This is a sequel to an earlier, more theoretical book, *The Child's Construction of Knowledge: Piaget for Teaching Children,* by George Forman and David Kuschner. *Constructive Play* is a practical guide containing over a hundred simple games and activities based on Piaget's theory of child development. The games and activities are open-ended allowing children to design their own rules, play at their own pace and develop an awareness of their own actions and attitudes about the real world.

The games are designed for ages two through four, but can be easily adapted for older children.

THE CREATIVE CURRICULUM FOR EARLY CHILDHOOD (Third Edition). Diane Trister Dodge and Laura J. Colker. Washington, DC: Teaching Strategies, Inc., 1992. Distributed by Gryphon House, Mt. Rainier, MD.

This is a comprehensive, child development-based curriculum that shows teachers how to create an effective learning environment for preschool and kindergarten children. The book describes a practical curriculum framework that allows teachers to be creative and flexible in building a program based on children's interests and strengths.

The Creative Curriculum organizes the learning environment into interest areas. For each area, it provides and explains a clear underlying rationale, goals and learning objectives for the children, the teacher's role, the parent's role and the process of setting up the physical environment to support child-centered learning. There are also video and slide tapes available to support the text.

DEVELOPMENTALLY APPROPRIATE PRACTICE IN EARLY CHILDHOOD PROGRAMS SERVING CHILDREN FROM BIRTH THROUGH AGE 8 (Expanded Edition). Sue Bredekamp, Editor. New York: National Association for the Education of Young Children, 1987.

This book provides a careful and thorough study of appropriate and inappropriate teaching practices for children from infancy through eight years old. Separate chapters address different ages. The chapters describing practices for ages 4-8 have been very helpful for many schools in changing their teaching approaches.

A GUIDE TO PROGRAM DEVELOPMENT FOR KINDERGARTEN PART I & II. Principle Editor Part I: Velma A. Adams. Principle Editor Part II: Donald G. Goranson. Connecticut State Board of Education, 1988. Available through Curriculum Unit, Bureau of Curriculum and Instruction, State Department of Education, P.O. Box 2219, Hartford, CT 06145.

An excellent, comprehensive and well written curriculum and program guide for teachers creating developmentally appropriate kindergarten programs. Both volumes are important resources in understanding the theory behind such an approach to teaching and the practical how-to's in implementing it.

I LEARN FROM CHILDREN. Caroline Pratt. New York: Harper & Row, 1990. (First Edition - 1948). Out of Print. Only available through Northeast Foundation for Children, Greenfield, MA.

Caroline Pratt first proposed the notion that children's play was their work. Like developmentalists today, she believed that education should fit the child and come from the child's experiences in the real world. This educational classic is the story of her philosophy in action through the chronicles of her school, City and Country. Creator of the standard unit block, Caroline Pratt shows how blocks become the medium for an integrated social studies curriculum in the primary grades.

THE LEARNING CHILD. Dorothy H. Cohen, New York: Pantheon Books, 1972.

A classic (and often overlooked) book by a leading expert in teacher education. Contains important theory and lots of practical advice in child development for parents and teachers alike. Written with clarity and deep feeling.

PLACES TO START: IMPLEMENTING THE DEVELOPMENTAL CLASSROOM (a VHS video). Marlynn K. Clayton. Greenfield, MA: Northeast Foundation for Children, 1989.

Adapted from a slide show, this video gives life to the developmentally effective practices used at the Greenfield Center School, NEFC's laboratory school. It includes a solid overview of philosophy, approaches to teaching and many practical ideas to use in the K-3 classroom. It explores classroom organization, age-appropriate materials, important management techniques, and ways children plan and evaluate their work at school.

PRIMARY RESOURCE HANDBOOK: For Kindergarten and First Grade. Compiled by Christine H. Kamp and Karen E. DeRusha. Newton, MA: Newton Public Schools, 1983.

The end product of a Mini-Leave Grant, this very detailed curriculum resource shares a wealth of information for teaching from a developmental perspective. Each section (art, music, dramatic play, blocks, language arts, etc.) provides a philosophy, resources and possible activities. Written for the Newton Public Schools, some of it is specific to that system.

PROMOTING COGNITIVE GROWTH. A DEVELOPMENTAL-INTERACTIONAL POINT OF VIEW. Barbara Biber, Edna Shapiro, David Wickens, Bank Street College of Education. Washington, DC: NAEYC, 1971.

A clear and readable account of teacher interaction with preschool children, focusing on the development of cognitive strength.

SCHOOLS WITHOUT FAILURE. William Glasser, M.D. New York: Harper & Row, 1969.

The much used approach to classroom discipline based on "reality therapy." Offers many important strategies for teachers.

TEACHER. Sylvia Ashton-Warner. New York: Bantam, 1971.

Of *Teacher*, Sir Herbert Read wrote: "Without exaggeration, it may be said that the author has discovered a way of saving humanity from self-destruction." An uplifting book for anyone in the profession.

Reading, Writing, Spelling
(Also see Resources, page 41)

THE ART OF TEACHING WRITING. Lucy McCormick Calkins. Portsmouth, NH: Heinemann, 1986.

This beautifully written book explores essential practices in teaching writing and offers sensitive insights into children as learners and thinkers. It contains excellent discussions of writing development, writing conferences, and reading-writing connections.

THE BEGINNINGS OF WRITING. Charles A. Temple, Ruth G. Nathan and Nancy A. Burris. Boston: Allyn and Bacon, 1982.

Subtitled, "A practical guide to a young child's discovery of writing through the scribbling, spelling and composing stages," this book is just that: practical. Teachers at any level stand to gain from this book, but those implementing a writing program in kindergarten or primary grades will find it most useful. Chapter Seven, "Making Progress in Spelling," contains a clear definition of the stages of spelling development.

CHOOSING BOOKS FOR KIDS. Joanne Oppenheim, Barbara Brenner, Betty Broegenhold. New York: Ballantine (A Bank Street Book), 1986.

This book offers comprehensive reviews of over 1,500 titles. It addresses children's development and its impact on book choice and reading response.

CLASSROOM STRATEGIES THAT WORK. Ruth Nathan, Frances Temple, Kathleen Juntunen, and Charles Temple. Portsmouth, NH: Heinemann, 1989.

The authors offer many practical suggestions for implementing process writing approach in the elementary school classroom. The book contains detailed examples of focus lessons and useful tools to support peer revising and editing.

THE CRAFT OF CHILDREN'S WRITING. Judith Newman. Portsmouth, NH: Heinemann, 1984.

This brief, easily read text explores young children's writing through examples of scribbles, drawings, and early lettering attempts.

THE EARLY DETECTION OF READING DIFFICULTIES (3rd Edition). Marie Clay. Portsmouth, NH: Heinemann, 1985.

This book is an invaluable resource for assisting slowly developing readers. It provides information on the systematic observation of young children's responses to classroom reading instruction and contains a set of Reading Recovery procedures for use in an early intervention program.

EVALUATION: WHOLE LANGUAGE, WHOLE CHILD. Jane Baskwill and Paulette Whitman. New York: Scholastic, 1988.

This book explores observation as an effective alternative to traditional testing. It contains many practical suggestions for recording and evaluating children's progress.

FOR READING OUT LOUD! A GUIDE TO SHARING BOOKS WITH CHILDREN. Margaret Mary Kimmel and Elizabeth Segel. New York: Delacorte Press, 1983.

A useful guide for parents and teachers. Contains hundreds of suggested readings at all age levels.

THE FOUNDATIONS OF LITERACY. Don Holdaway. Portsmouth, NH: Heinemann, 1979.

This classic volume discusses historical and current reading practices, literacy before school, and the shared book experience.

IDEAS AND INSIGHTS. Dorothy Watson, ed. Urbana, IL: NCTE, 1987.

Hundreds of teachers offer valuable suggestions for activities that support reading, writing, listening, and speaking across the curriculum.

INDEPENDENCE IN READING (2nd Edition). Don Holdaway. Portsmouth, NH: Heinemann, 1980.

This book contains excellent suggestions for implementing an independent reading program. The information on conferencing, developing reading skills and strategies, and recordkeeping and evaluation is invaluable for teachers using any type of literature-based reading program.

INSTANT READERS SERIES. Bill Martin, Jr. and Peggy Brogan. New York: Holt, Rhinehart, and Winston, Inc., 1972.

Delightful books for young readers who will read and remember them for a long time. Excellent for kindergarten or prekindergarten library.

IN THE MIDDLE: WRITING, READING, AND LEARNING WITH ADOLESCENTS. Nancie Atwell. Portsmouth, NH: Heinemann, 1987.

This book tells the story of Atwell's experiences as an eight-grade teacher in Boothbay Harbor, Maine. It describes her transition from running a fairly traditional junior high English classroom to creating a workshop where junior high readers and writers engage in literate and literary dialogues. There are very useful appendices with specific lists of materials, books, questions, and topics Atwell has found successful.

INVESTIGATE NONFICTION. Donald Graves. Portsmouth, NH: Heinemann, 1989.

This book explores ways to help children develop their own nonfiction voice as they examine the world around them and report on what they know (also *Experiment with Fiction).*

INVITATIONS: CHANGING AS TEACHERS AND LEARNERS K-12. Regie Routman. Portsmouth, NH: Heinemann, 1991.

This is an invaluable, practical, easy-to-read text that has been written to support and encourage all K-12 educators who want more specific information on putting whole language theory into practice. Routman begins this book where *Transitions,* her first book, left off. It provides a remarkably complete and well-organized resource that will help make whole language teaching and learning possible for everyone.

Chapters are complete within themselves and can be read in any order to suit the teacher's needs. Also included are lists of recommended literature for K-12, professional books, journal articles and literacy extension resources.

LITERACY THROUGH LITERATURE. Terry Johnson and Daphne Louis. Portsmouth, NH: Heinemann, 1987.

The authors present hundreds of ideas for using children's literature as the basis of the classroom language program. They describe activities designed to help children explore character, plot, setting, and theme in varied and meaningful ways.

LIVING BETWEEN THE LINES. Lucy McCormick Calkins with Shelley Harwayne. Portsmouth, NH: Heinemann, 1991.

This publication offers valuable insights into the use of writers' notebooks and rehearsal for writing. It also examines reading-writing connections and their effect on children's writing of memoir, picture books, and non-fiction.

ON LEARNING TO READ. Bruno Bettelheim and Karen Zelan. New York: Vintage Books, 1981.

The noted child psychologist examines approaches to reading in relationship to school and development.

THE NEWREAD ALOUD HANDBOOK (Revised Edition). Jim Trelease. New York: Penguin Books (Viking Press), 1989.

A marvelous resource bibliography by a journalist who speaks plainly to parents and teachers.

READ ON: A CONFERENCE APPROACH TO READING. David Hornsby and Deborah Sukarna with Jo-Ann Parry. Portsmouth, NH: Heinemann, 1986.

The authors offer a practical guide to reading through literature. The ideas for conferencing, conferencing questions, and response activities are particularly useful (also *Write On* by Parry & Hornsby).

READING MISCUE INVENTORY. Yetta Goodman, Dorothy Watson, and Carolyn Burke. New York: Richard C. Owen, 1987.

The authors offer detailed descriptions of an assessment strategy that offers teachers a "window on the reading process" and, at the same time, helps them observe and understand their students' reading.

READING PROCESS AND PRACTICE. Constance Weaver. Portsmouth, NH: Heinemann, 1988.

The author explores socio-psycholinguistic theory in a very understandable manner. She integrates theory into a practical presentation of a whole language approach to reading.

THE SOUNDS OF LANGUAGE. Bill Martin, Jr. with Peggy Brogan & John Archaumbault. Allen, TX: DLM, 1990.

An updated version of the classic reading program that pays attention to and makes sense of the developmental interests of children. Making use of songs, poems, legends, good literature and "Noodles," the entire program is a joyful testament to childhood. The Teachers' Guide is inspiring reading and honors the professional intelligence of the teacher. Bill Martin, himself, is a master workshop leader who understands the relationship between development and reading.

SPEL...IS A FOUR LETTER WORD. Richard Gentry. Portsmouth, NH: Heinemann, 1987.

Gentry considers how or why spelling education may interfere with the process of learning to spell.

TOWARDS A READING-WRITING CLASSROOM. Andrea Butler and Jan Turbill. Portsmouth, NH: Heinemann, 1987.

The authors discuss the theory and practice of working with children in a process-oriented classroom. Many valuable suggestions for curriculum, classroom organization, and scheduling are offered.

TRANSITIONS: FROM LITERATURE TO LITERACY. Regie Routman. Portsmouth, NH: Heinemann, 1988.

Regie Routman shares the story of her transition from a basal to a literature-based reading program. Her discussion offers support and practical suggestions for teachers involved in a similar change process.

WHAT DID I WRITE? Marie Clay. Portsmouth, NH: Heinemann, 1975.

This book examines children's first efforts to write. The author traces patterns of development in actual examples of children's work.

WHAT'S WHOLE IN WHOLE LANGUAGE. Kenneth Goodman. Portsmouth, NH: Heinemann, 1986.

This brief, easily read text explores whole language as a teaching philosophy.

THE WHOLE LANGUAGE CATALOGUE. Kenneth Goodman, Lois Bridges Bird, and Yetta Goodman. Santa Rosa, CA: American School Publishers (Macmillan/McGraw Hill), 1990.

This Big Book for teachers is packed with ideas, strategies, resources, holistic theory and philosophy, language stories, and more.

WISHES, LIES AND DREAMS. Kenneth Koch. New York: Harper & Row, 1980.

This book offers teachers wonderful suggestions for inspiring children as poets.

WRITING: TEACHERS AND CHILDREN AT WORK: Donald H. Graves. Exeter, NH: Heinemann Educational Books, 1983.

A book for those who have followed the writing of Donald Graves and the work of the Writing Process Laboratory at the University of New Hampshire. Donald Graves has helped many teachers learn how to teach writing. The skill of conferencing with young writers is clearly described. Graves has many useful thoughts about classroom structure, too!

Mathematics

(Also see Resources, page 42)

CHILDREN'S MATHEMATICAL THINKING: A DEVELOPMENTAL FRAMEWORK FOR PRE-SCHOOL, PRIMARY, AND SPECIAL EDUCATION TEACHERS. Arthur Baroody. New York: Teachers College Press, 1987.

This book describes a practical framework for understanding children's mathematical thinking and the difficulties some children may encounter in their mathematical development. This discussion of the constructivist approach helps teachers use children's errors to discover root causes of conceptual difficulties.

DEVELOPING NUMBER CONCEPTS USING UNIFIX®️ CUBES. Kathy Richardson. Reading, MA: Addison-Wesley, 1984.

A book of concrete activities to help children develop number concepts using readily available Unifix cubes as the tool. It is organized around standard primary mathematical objectives and an assessment program is provided for each objective. Classroom organizational techniques are also addressed throughout the book.

FAMILY MATH. Jean Kerr Stenmark, Virginia Thompson, Ruth Cossey. Berkeley, CA: Lawrence Hall of Science, University of California, 1986. Also available in Spanish.

Written for parents and children to do math together at home or at school in Family Math classes, the over 90 "hands-on" activities are also excellent for classroom use. The book covers word problems, logical thinking, number exploration, measurement, probability, estimation, geometry, spatial thinking and use of calculators.

GROUP GAMES IN EARLY EDUCATION. Constance Kamii and Rheta DeVries. Washington, DC: National Association for the Education of Young Children, 1980.

This book explores the application of Piaget's theory of constructivism to children's group games. It shows what children can learn in these games and how teachers can intervene in ways that maximize children's learning. Concrete examples of games and teachers' actions are provided as well as a discussion of the issue of competition in games.

LIVING AND LEARNING MATHEMATICS: STORIES AND STRATEGIES FOR SUPPORTING MATHEMATICAL LITERACY. David Whitin, Heidi Mills, and Timothy O'Keefe. Portsmouth, NH: Heinemann, 1990.

The authors discuss ways children gain an understanding of their world by using mathematics for meaningful purposes. Children's work is used to illustrate the kinds of strategies six year olds devise as they solve mathematical problems.

MATHEMATICS THEIR WAY. Mary Baratta-Lorton. Reading, MA: Addison-Wesley Publishing, 1976.

This book is a valuable tool to develop understanding and insight into the patterns of mathematics through the use of concrete materials. It is a complete and extremely useful guide for teachers which includes philosophy, preparation of materials, student and teacher records, assessment of skills and parent education. The activities were designed for K-grade 3.

MATHS IN CONTEXT: A THEMATIC APPROACH. Deidre Edwards. Portsmouth, NH: Heinemann, 1990.

From Australia comes a lovely little book showing a thematic approach to the teaching of mathematics. Both the thematic process and detailed units are presented.

SAXON MATH K-3. Nancy Larson. Norman, OK: Saxon Publishers, 1991.

This is an exciting new math curriculum from John Saxon's group. It is based on the theory that mastery and long-term retention of mathematical concepts come from an incremental and repetitive approach to learning in math. This curriculum provides practice every day of all concepts previously introduced. The program relies heavily on manipulatives and requires children's active, "hands-on" physical participation as well as mental and oral participation. The program is designed for heterogeneously grouped students.

WORKJOBS. Mary Baratta-Lorton, Reading, MA: Addison-Wesley Publishing, 1972.

This book is based on the learning tasks designed and used with young children in Mary Baratta-Lorton's classroom. The activities all involve manipulation of objects around one concept. The activities involve perception, matching, classification, sounds and letters, sets, numbers, sequences, combining and separating groups and relationships. The preparation of each activity, classroom routine and record keeping systems are thoroughly explained. This is a good book to begin with to set up active learning centers.

Other books in this series are: *Workjobs...for Parents,* by Mary Baratta-Lorton, 1975; and *Workjobs II,* by Mary Baratta-Lorton, 1979. This last book focuses on number activities for kindergarten and grades 1 and 2.

WYNROTH MATH PROGRAMS. Lloyd Wynroth. P.O. Box 578, Ithaca, NY 14850.

A *deductive* math program that follows a game format, teaching math concepts through game rules. Very appropriate developmentally.

YOUNG CHILDREN REINVENT ARITHMETIC: IMPLICATIONS OF PIAGET'S THEORY. Constance Kazulo Kamii. New York: Teachers College Press. 1985.

For those interested in a constructivist approach to the acquisition of mathematical competence, this volume will prove illuminating. Jean Piaget discovered from his research that children learn arithmetic by constructing it from the inside, through their own thinking rather than by internalizing a set of rules from the outside. This book applies Piaget's work to real classroom teaching and demonstrates its validity and importance.

Kamii is also the author of *Children Continue to Reinvent Arithmetic, 2nd Grade: Implications of Piaget's Theory* (Teachers College Press, 1989).

Science and Social Studies

(Also see Resources, page 44)

THE BLOCK BOOK. Elisabeth S. Hirsch, editor. Washington, DC: NAEYC, 1974.

A collection of essays about the development of block building skills in children, the purpose and importance of block building in the classroom, and practical ideas for implementing block building into a school curriculum.

BLOCK BUILDING: SOME PRACTICAL SUGGESTIONS FOR TEACHERS. Maya Apelman. Boulder, CO: Boulder Valley Public Schools/Bank Street College Follow-Through Program, 1982. Available through the author at 755 Lincoln Place, Boulder, CO 80302

A small pamphlet that clearly addresses the development of block building skills in children and provides a wealth of practical information for teachers interested in implementing a block program.

DOING WHAT SCIENTISTS DO: CHILDREN LEARN TO INVESTIGATE THEIR WORLD. Ellen Doris. Portsmouth, NH: Heinemann Books and Northeast Foundation for Children, 1991. Available through Northeast Foundation for Children, Greenfield, MA.

This book translates the theory of "discovery science" into a practical, step-by-step approach that all teachers can implement. It shows teachers how to begin and continue a science program; how to help children feel interested in their world and able to find out about it; how to organize and manage the classroom in a way that encourages interest and productive work; and how to deal with children's differing needs. It includes lots of children's work and dialogue and an extensive list of resources.

DRAMATIC PLAY: AN INTEGRATED CURRICULUM GUIDE. Karen DeRusha. Lexington, MA: Early Education Curriculum, 1990. Available through Northeast Foundation for Children, Greenfield, MA.

This is an excellent resource to help teachers and PreK-2 students create a "housekeeping" area that encourages dynamic, productive, and intellectually stimulating play. DeRusha shares specific ideas about theme development, theme content, the organizaton and management of a dramatic play area with furniture and props, and the integration of dramatic play into other areas of the curriculum.

The book presents a clear rationale for incorporating dramatic play into children's learning, lists goals for teaching dramatic play, and explains the positive connection between dramatic play and cognitive development. Includes a bibliography and materials for reproduction.

ELEMENTARY SCIENCE STUDY (ESS) CURRICULUM (teacher guides). Newton, MA: Educational Development Center. Available through Delta Education, Inc., Hudson, NH.

The most well known of all "discovery" curricula, ESS contains over fifty individual units created for the teaching of science, math and social studies in the elementary grades. There exists no better single source for creative ideas and activities in the field of developmental curricula. Begun in 1960 with immense support from the National Science Foundation, ESS is a monument to the best in American teaching.

Some of the individual units available and appropriate for primary use are: ATTRIBUTE GAMES AND PROBLEMS, BATTERIES AND BULBS, CLAY BOATS, COLORED SOLUTIONS, EARTHWORMS, EGGS AND TADPOLES, GROWING SEEDS, MYSTERY POWDERS, PENDULUMS, PRIMARY BALANCING, and SINK OR FLOAT.

I LEARN FROM CHILDREN. Caroline Pratt. New York: Harper & Row, 1990. (First Edition-1984). Out of Print. Only available through Northeast Foundation for Children, Greenfield, MA.

See description under Development in the Classroom section.

LEARNING AND LOVING IT: THEME STUDIES IN THE CLASSROOM. Ruth Gamberg, et al. Portsmouth, NH: Heinemann, 1988.

Beneficial to teachers currently using thematic approaches as well as for those just getting started. Documents the real life of themes, plus a clear account of theme process from beginning to end.

SAND & WATER. Seddon Kelly Beaty and Karen DeRusha. Lexington, MA: Early Education Curriculum, 1987. Available through Northeast Foundation for Children, Greenfield, MA.

Sand and water are great fun for children, but they're important educational tools as well. Beaty and DeRusha explain the benefits of sand and water activities, identify discrete stages of sand and water play, outline the role of the teacher, and include a wealth of multidisciplinary activities that expand on basic play — language arts, reading, art, music, and audio/video.

The book covers table placement, cleanup and storage, rules of behavior, sink-and-float activities, sand timers, and more. Includes illustrations and an extensive bibliography.

SCIENCE FOR ALL AMERICANS. F. James Rutherford and Andrew Ahlgren. New York/Oxford: Oxford University Press, 1990.

This remarkable book for teachers and administrators on math and science education begins with this powerful statement: "Education has no higher purpose than preparing people to lead personally fulfilling and responsible lives." Drafted by the American Association for the Advancement of Science, the book is not a curriculum, but a powerful treatise on what should be taught, and includes some consideration of how it should be taught.

TEACHING PRIMARY SCIENCE (teacher guides). Chelsea College Project. Chelsea, England: 1976. Available through Teacher's Laboratory, Brattleboro, VT.

A developmental approach to Primary Science based on the work of Dorothy Diamond and others in England. Contains excellent bibliographies and teachers' guides which include such titles as AERIAL MODELS, CANDLES, FIBERS AND FABRICS, MIRRORS AND MAGNIFIERS, MUSICAL INSTRUMENTS, PAINTS AND MATERIALS, SCIENCE FROM WATERPLAY, SCIENCE FROM WOOD and SEEDS AND SEEDLINGS.

YOUNG GEOGRAPHERS: HOW THEY EXPLORE THE WORLD AND HOW THEY MAP THE WORLD. Lucy Sprague Mitchell. New York: Bank Street College of Education, 1991 (First Edition-1934). Available through Northeast Foundation for Children, Greenfield, MA.

One of the few truly developmental approaches to the teaching of geography and social studies. Succinct and clearly written. Makes as much sense today as it did in 1934, if not more. Contains both a theoretical base and developmental sequences as well as practical ideas and lessons. Delightful vintage photographs show active classrooms of fifty years ago.

Catalogues

These are some of the catalogues that offer excellent materials and teacher resources to support and enrich an activity-based, developmentally appropriate classroom. Specific items of interest are noted.

AMERICAN GUIDANCE SERVICE, INC., Publishers Building, Circle Pines, MN 55014-1796 — 1-800-328-2560
- Carries the Social Skills Rating System and Social Skills Intervention Guide, an excellent assessment tool for measuring children's social skills and a classroom's social curriculum (see *Caring to Learn*, in Social Curriculum section of Bibliography)

CHASELLE, INC./NEW ENGLAND SCHOOL SUPPLY, 9645 Gerwig Lane, Columbia, MD 21046-1503 — 1-800-242-7355
- Good, basic classroom materials

COMMUNITY PLAYTHINGS, Rte. 213, Rifton, NY 12471 — 1-800-777-4244
- Excellent quality wooden furniture, unit blocks, big blocks, block play accessories, dramatic play equipment

CREATIVE PUBLICATIONS, 5040 West 111th Street, Oak Lawn, IL 60453 — 1-800-624-0822
- Beautiful and interesting math manipulatives and games

CUISENAIRE COMPANY OF AMERICA, INC., 12 Church Street, New Rochelle, NY 10805
- Cuisenaire rods

DELTA EDUCATION: HANDS-ON SCIENCE AND HANDS-ON MATH, P.O. Box 950, Hudson, NH, 03051 — 1-800-442-5444
- Carries ESS and other hands-on science programs and teaching guides as well as science kits for theme study
- Offers Geoblocks and other excellent math materials

GRYPHON HOUSE, P.O. Box 275, Mt. Rainier, MD 20712 — 1-800-638-0928
- Early childhood teacher resources
- Children's literature
- Offers "Highlights; Gryphon House Teacher Exchange"

HEINEMANN EDUCATIONAL BOOKS, INC., 361 Hanover Street, Portsmouth, NH 03801 — 1-800-541-2086
- At the forefront for writing process and whole language resources, and now publishes books that extend that approach to other content areas

HIGHSCOPE PRESS, 600 N. River Street, Ypsilanti, MI 48198-2898 — 1-313-485-2000
- Excellent early childhood teacher resource materials including books, videos, films and film strips,
- Public policy, research and parent materials
- Offers "Highscope Resource: A Magazine for Educators"

INTERACT: LEARNING THROUGH INVOLVEMENT, P.O. Box 997-Y92, Lakeside, CA 92040 — 1-800-359-0961
- Excellent resoures for cooperative learning and integrated curriculum

KAPLAN SCHOOL SUPPLY CORPORATION, P.O. Box 609, Lewisville, NC 27023 — 1-800-334-2014
- Excellent variety of quality classroom materials and supplies
- Multicultural crayons and paints

LAKESHORE LEARNING MATERIALS, 2695 E. Dominguez Street., Carson, CA 90749 — 1-800-421-5354
- Clip-on Wheels and Clip-on Magnetic Hitches for unit block play as well as other quality accessories
- People Colors markers, crayons and paints
- Multi-ethnic puppet families, dolls and career puppets
- "Lakeshore Apartments" (apartment dollhouse)
- Great variety of quality materials

MODERN LEARNING PRESS AND PROGRAMS FOR EDUCATION, P.O. Box 167, Dept. 323, Rosemont, NJ 08556 — 1-800-627-5867
- Words I Use When I Write (For Grades 1-2) and More Words I Use When I Write (For Grades 3-4) — personal spelling guides that include commonly used words and lots of space for the child's own special words
- Gesell Kindergarten and School Age Assessment Materials

NAEYC EARLY CHILDHOOD RESOURCES CATALOG, 1509 16th Street NW, Washington, DC 20036-1426 — 1-800-424-2460
- Excellent and inexpensive teacher resource materials in books, brochures, posters, videos and conferences
- Offers subcription to bimonthly magazine, "Young Children" and to "Early Childhood Research Quarterly"

SUNRISE BOOKS, TAPES & VIDEOS, P.O. Box B, Provo, UT 84603 — 1-800-456-7770
- Quality teacher resources supporting a positive approach to discipline and classroom management

TEACHERS COLLEGE PRESS, Teachers College, Columbia University, New York, NY 10027. Address for placing orders: P.O. Box 2032, Colchester, VT 05449 — 1-800-445-6638
- Known for classics in the field of education
- Offers subscription to "Quarterly Journal of Teachers College"

TEACHERS' LABORATORY, P.O. Box 6480, Brattleboro, VT 05302 — 1-802-254-3457
- Their goal is to enrich math and science instruction with a combination of materials, equipment, publications and programs which directly assist teachers in offering dynamic, hands-on learning
- "Notes to Teachers" accompany most major items of equipment and some publications. Written by teachers, these "notes" give instructional support and outline both appropriate uses and specific activities
- Lots of materials that explore inventions, design, and technology
- Offers a subscription to a professional newsletter, "Connect"

ZEPHYR PRESS, P.O. Box 13448-NW, Tucson, AZ 85732-3448 — 1-602-322-5090
- Dedicated to translating new theories of learning and thinking (multiple intelligences, varied learning styles, right brain/left brain) into practical classroom approaches

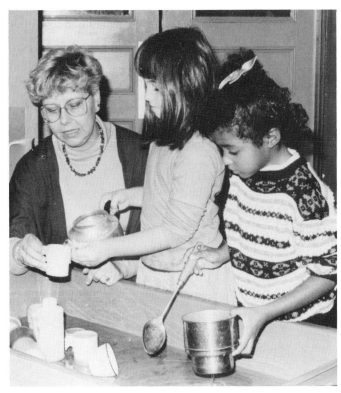